Flare

Art & Fashion

Adult Coloring Book

60 Illustrations

By : Mehwish Abbas
Website: www.mehwish.me

ISBN-13: 978-1540450845
ISBN-10: 1540450848

This coloring book belongs to the awesome

_____

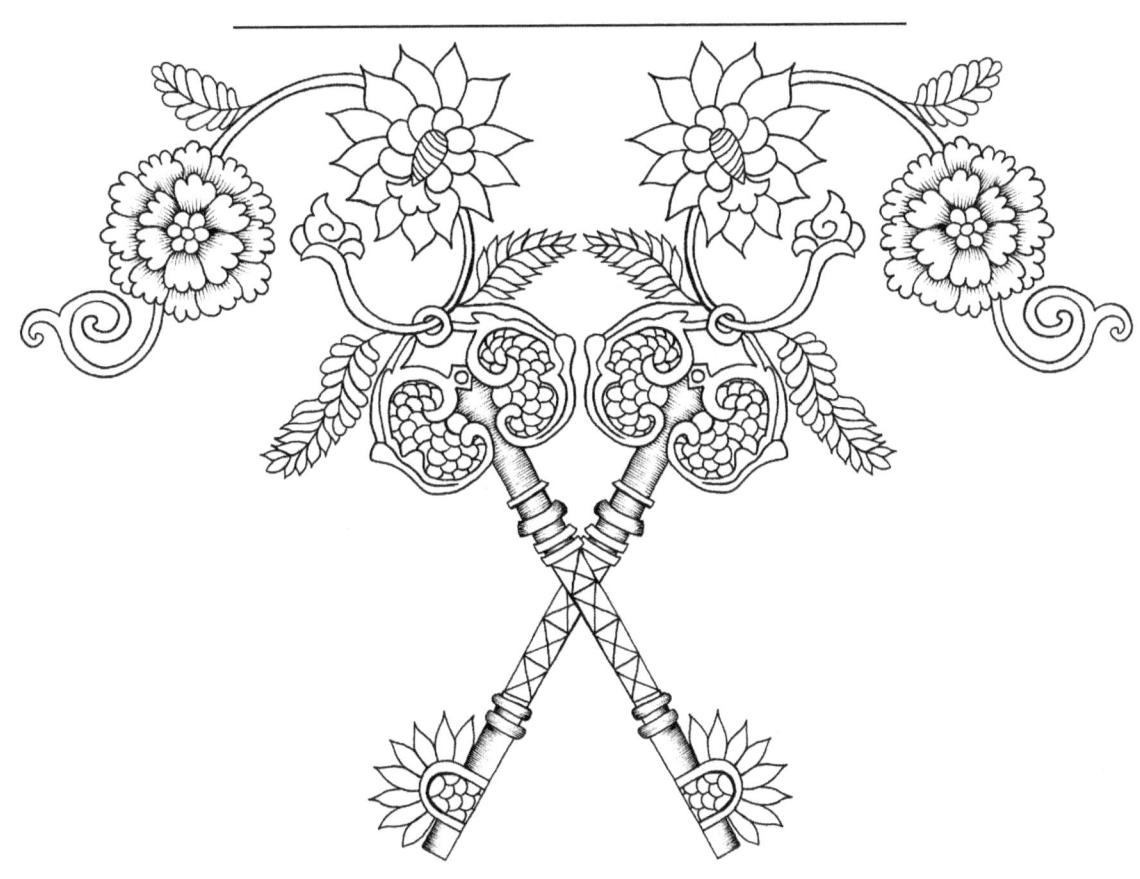

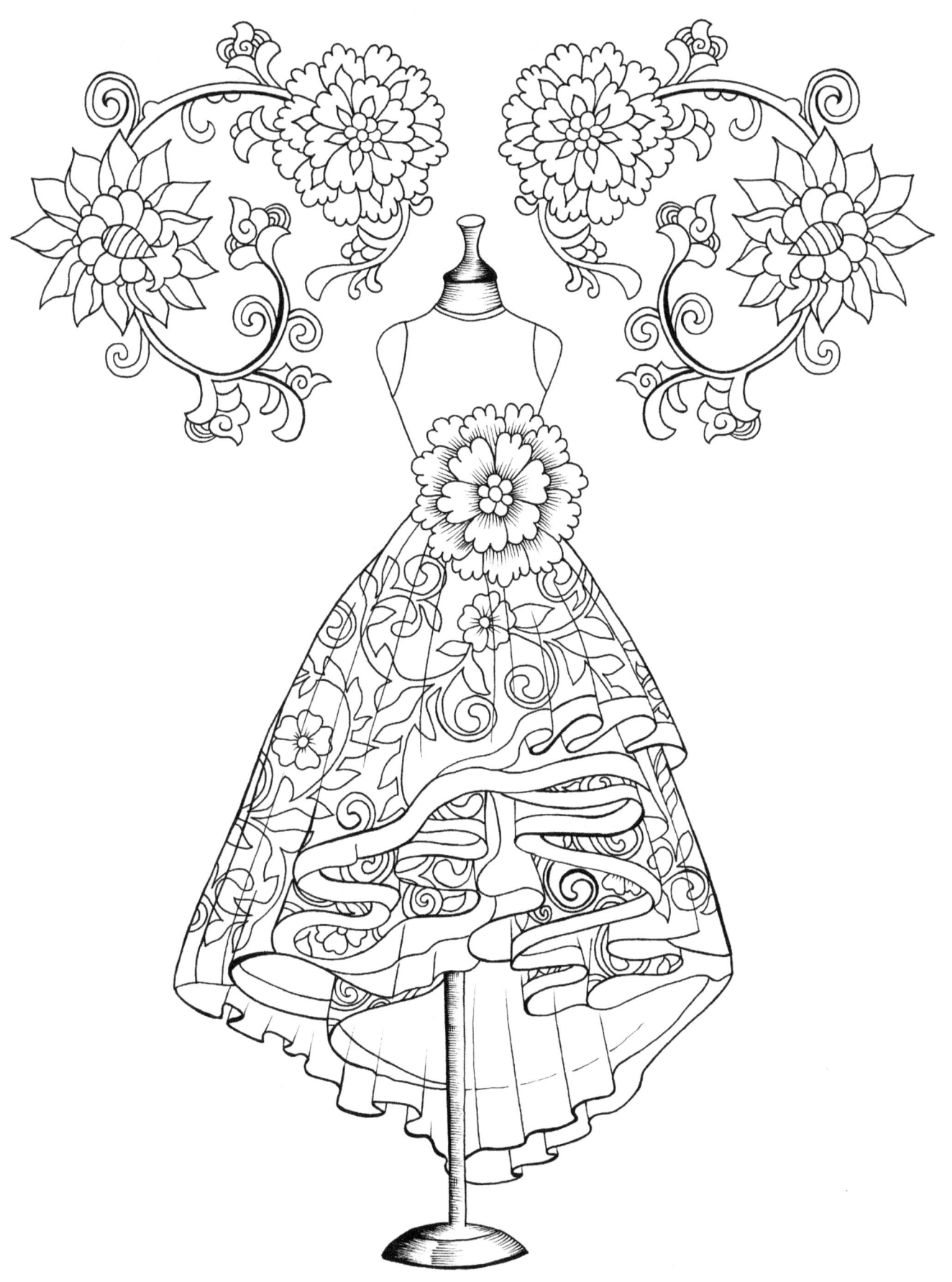

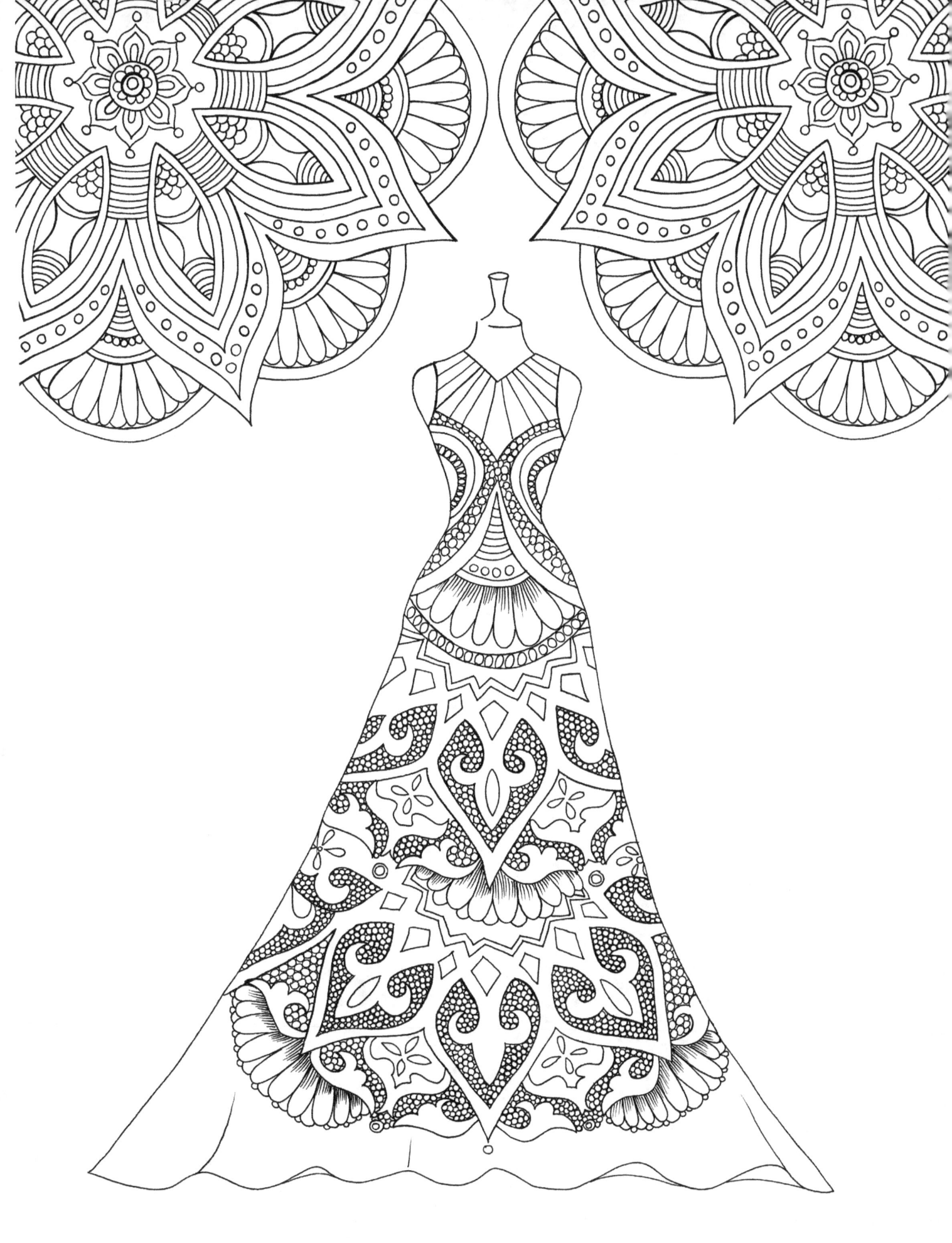

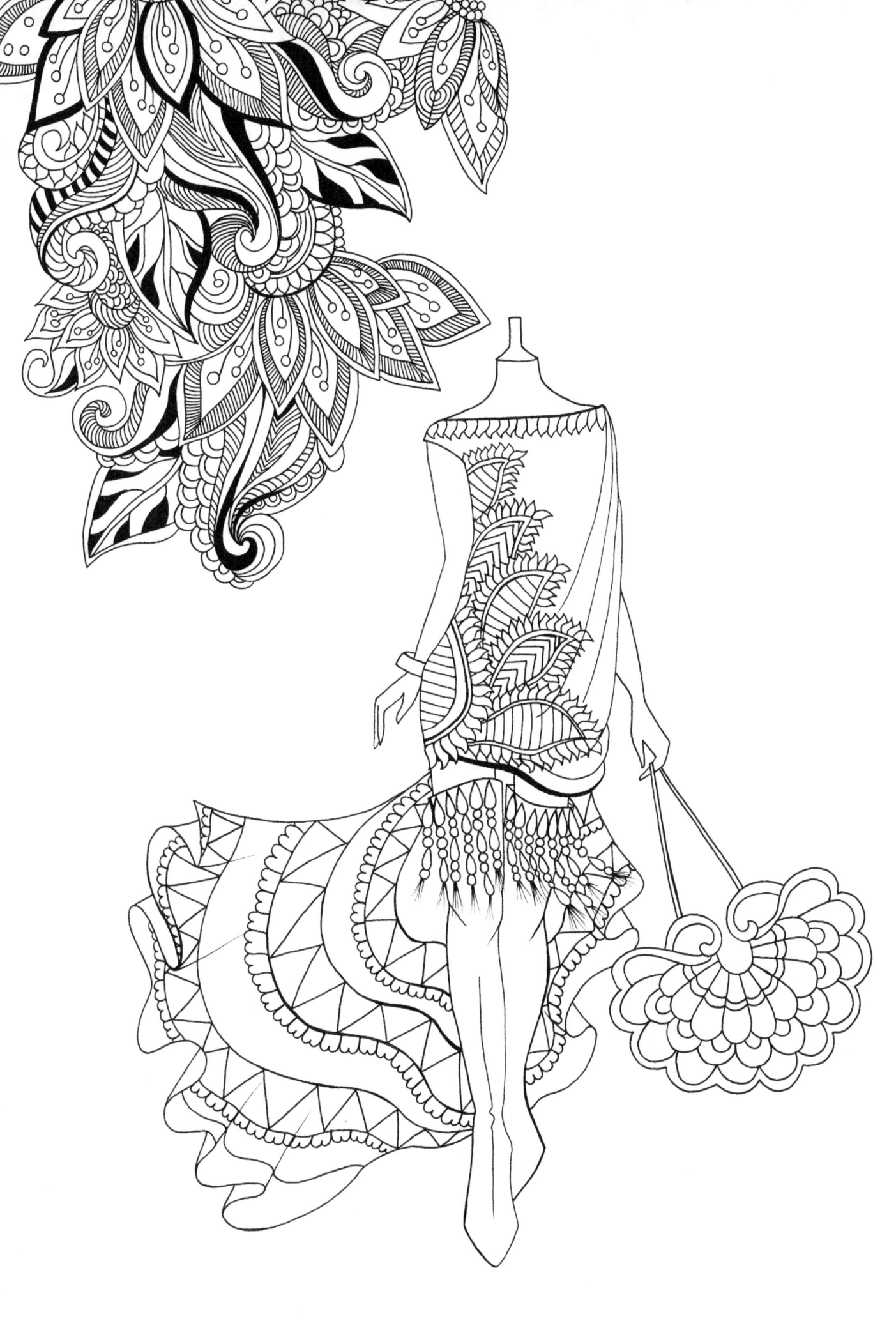

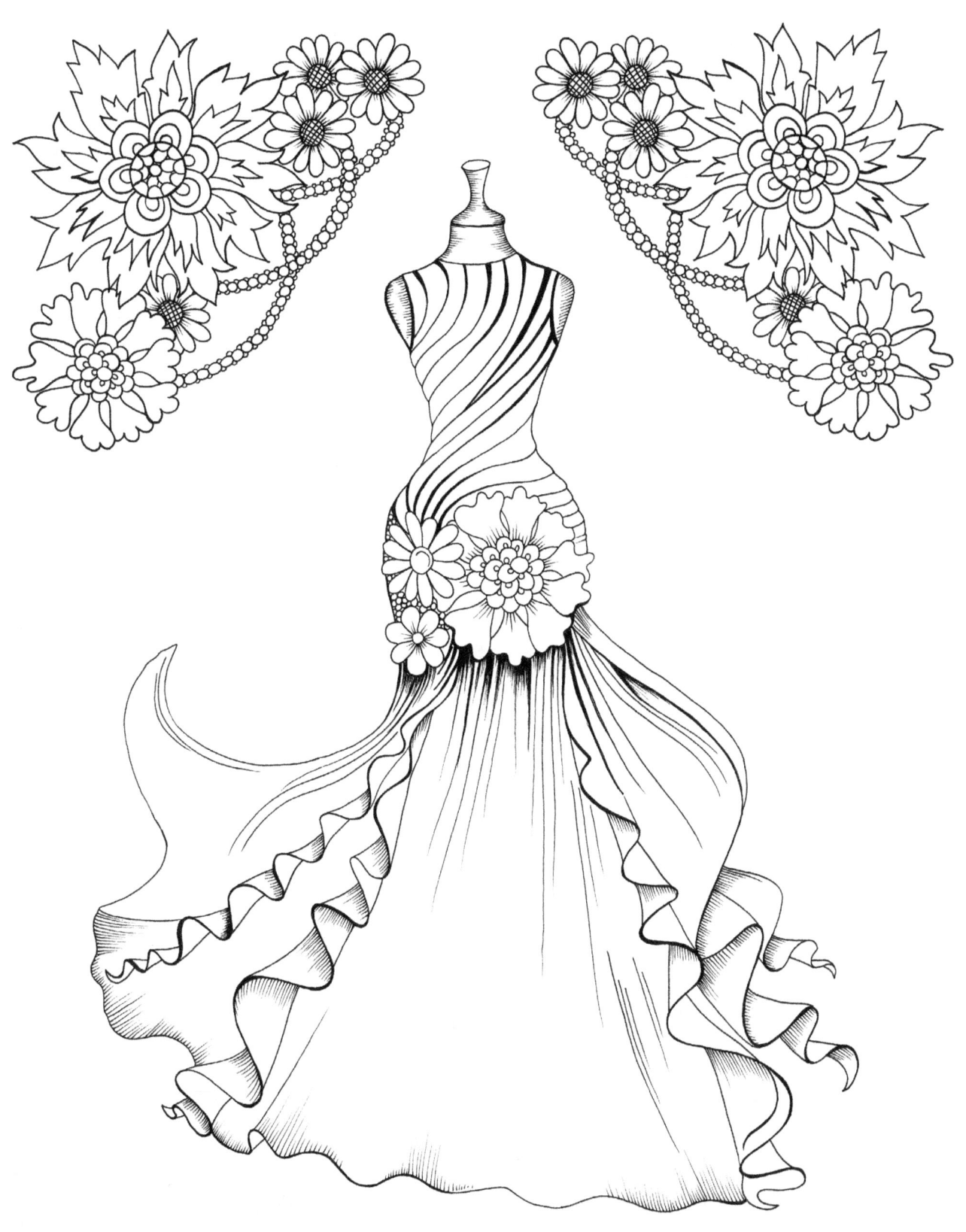

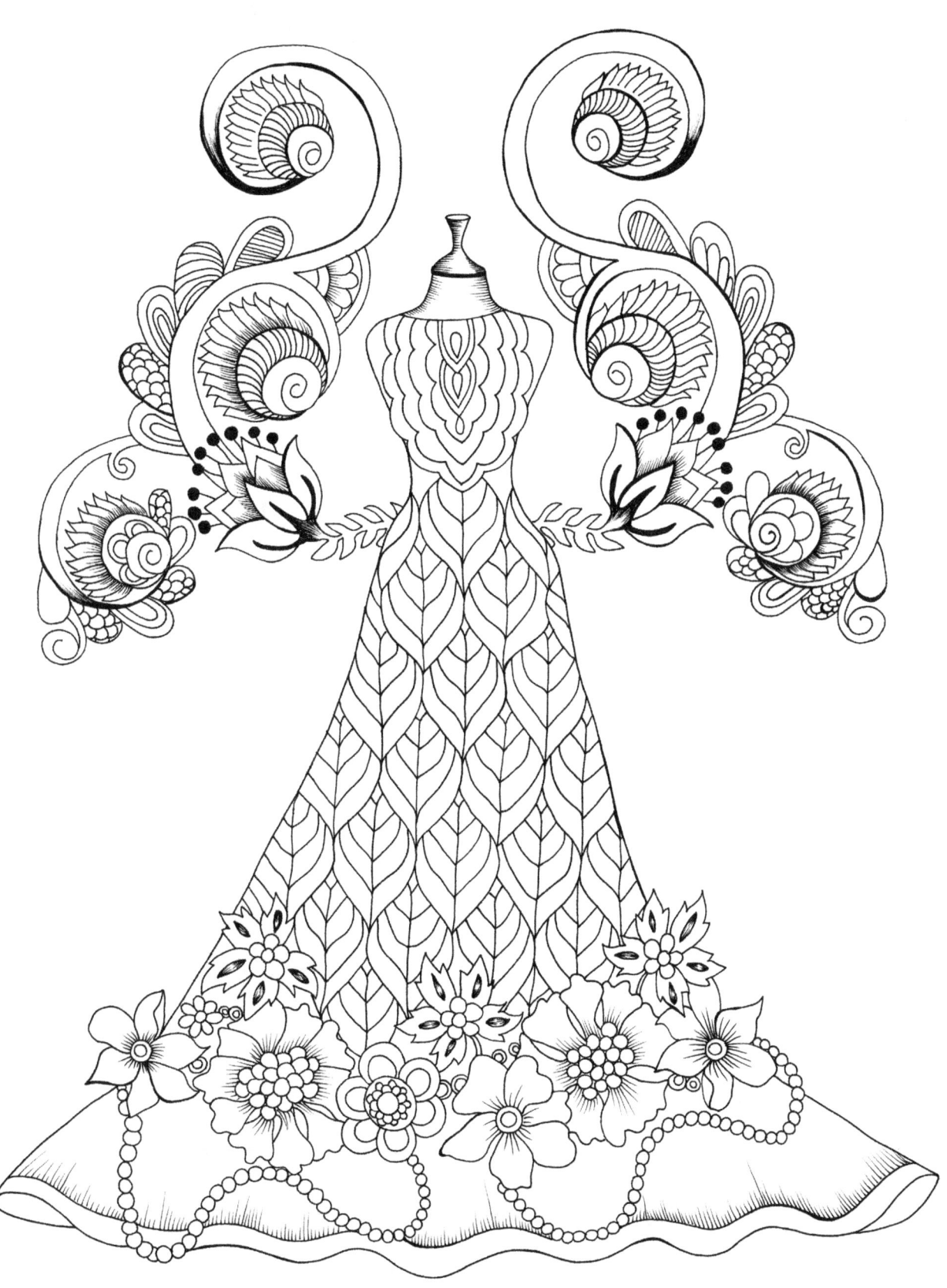

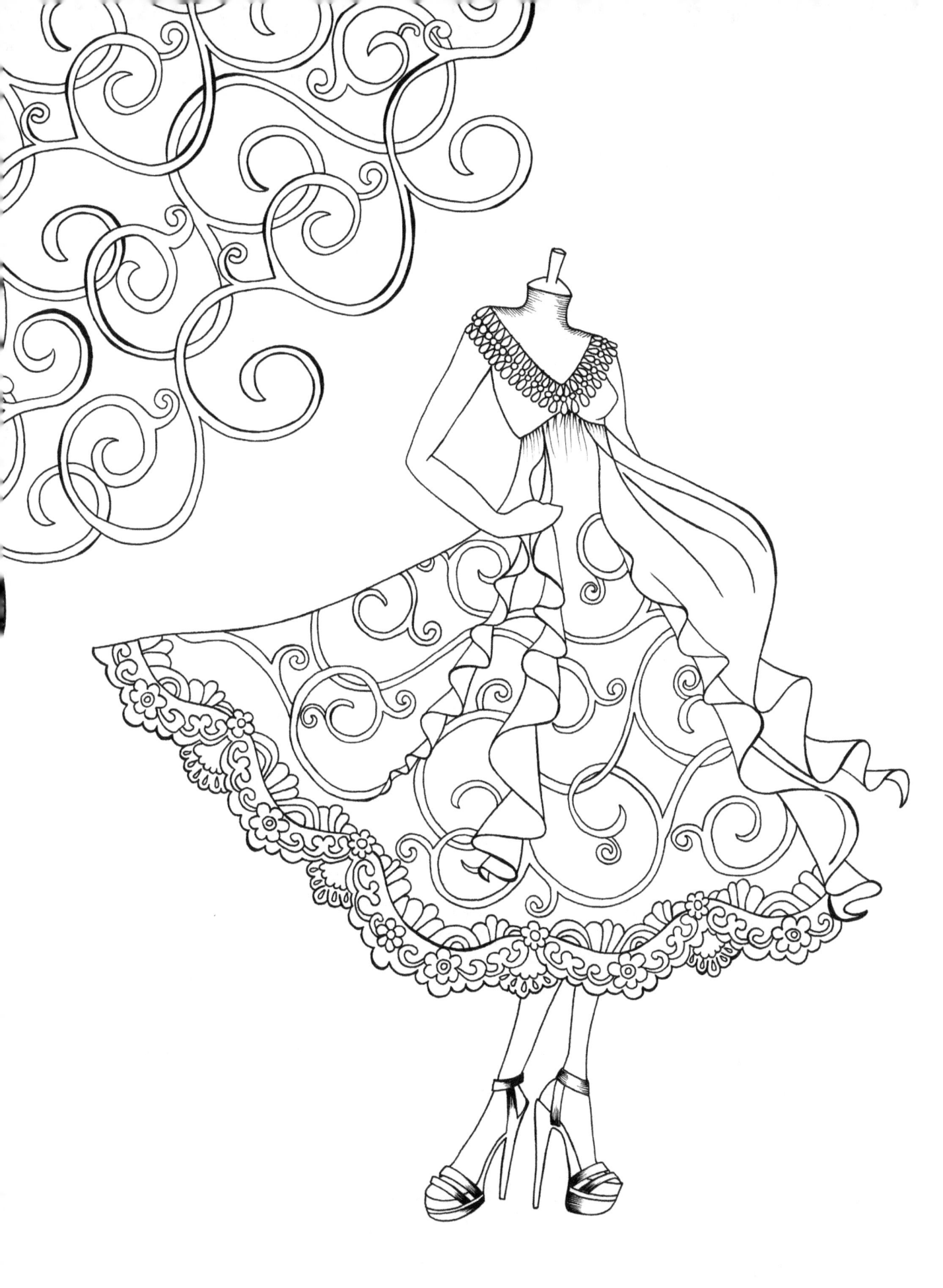

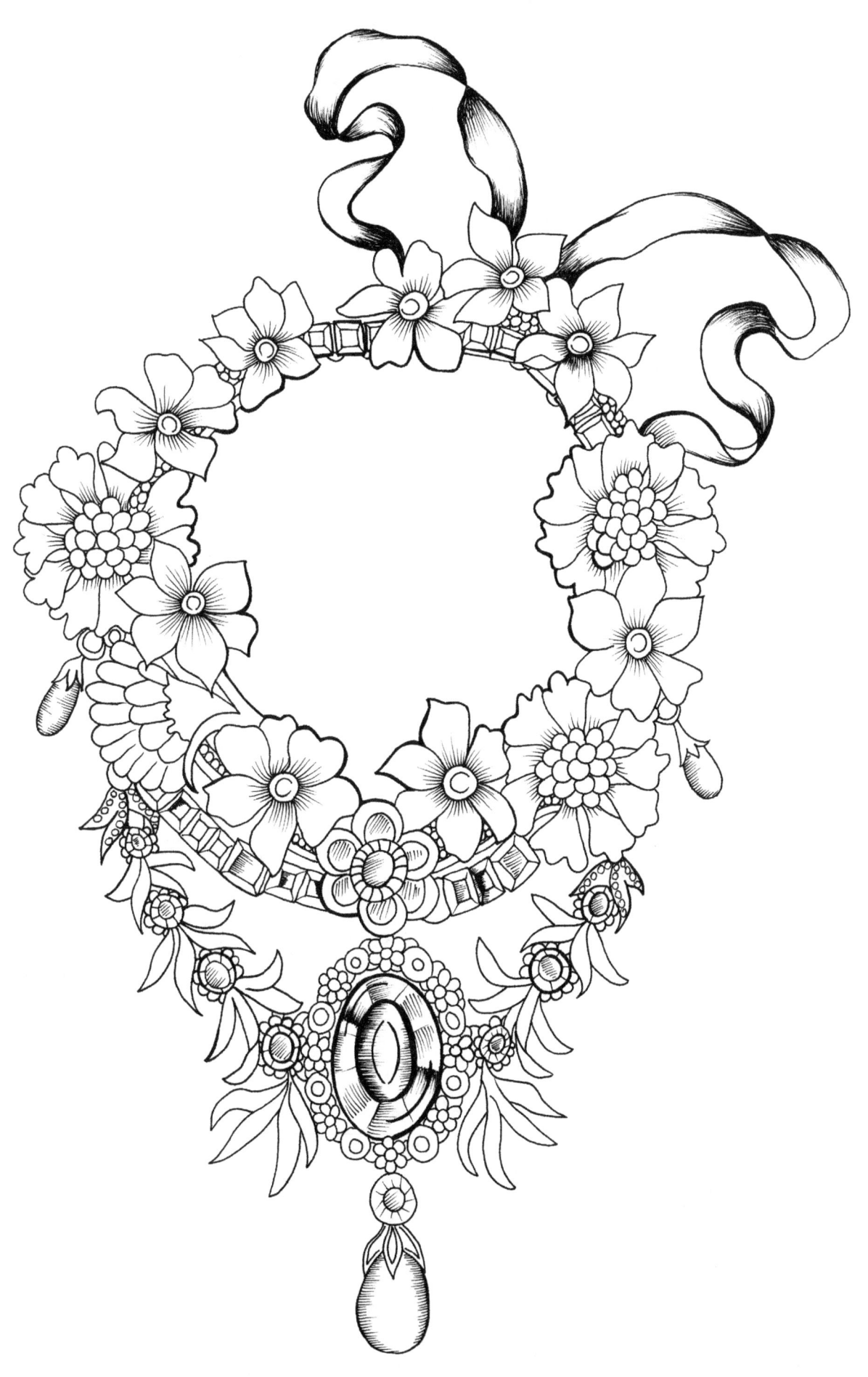

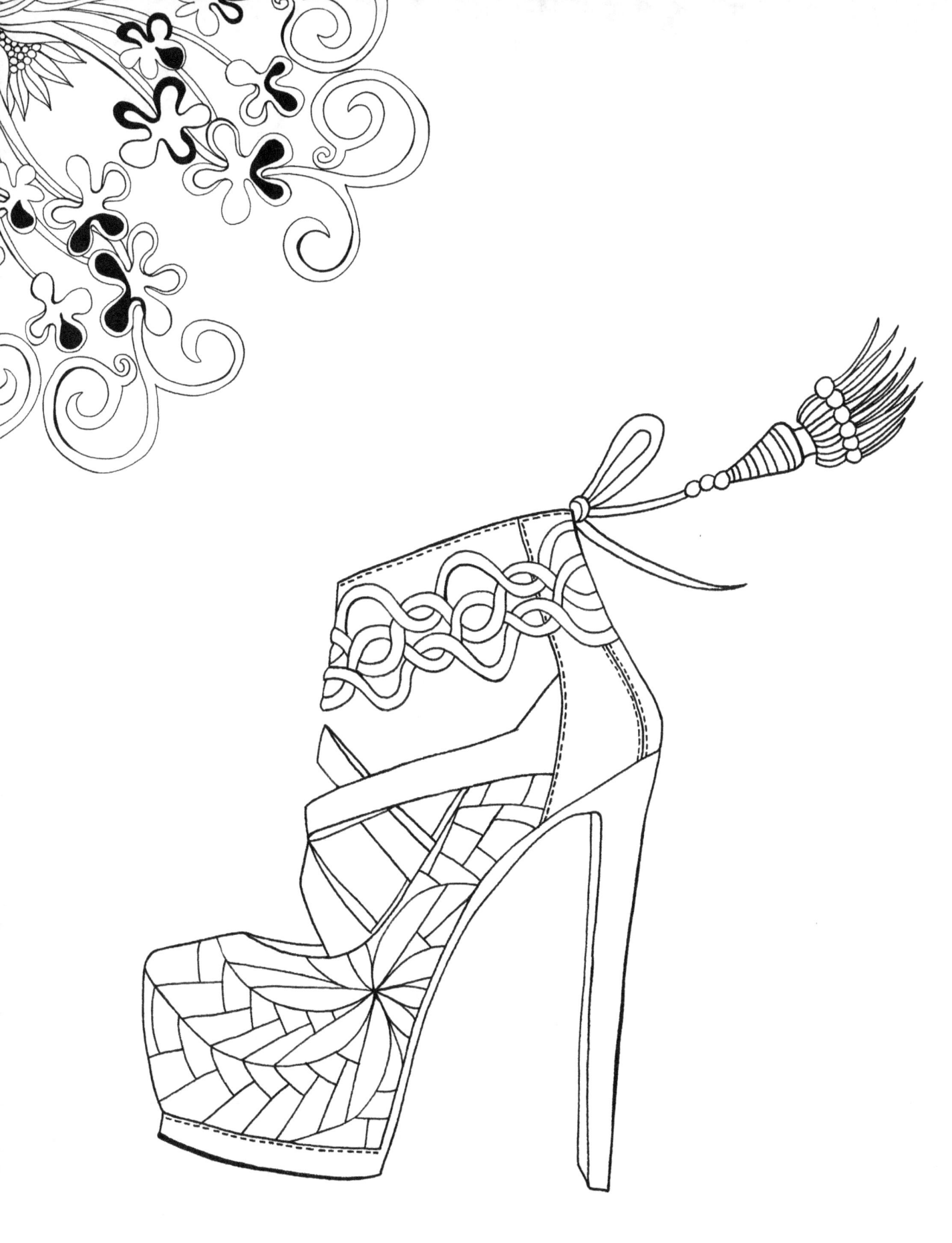

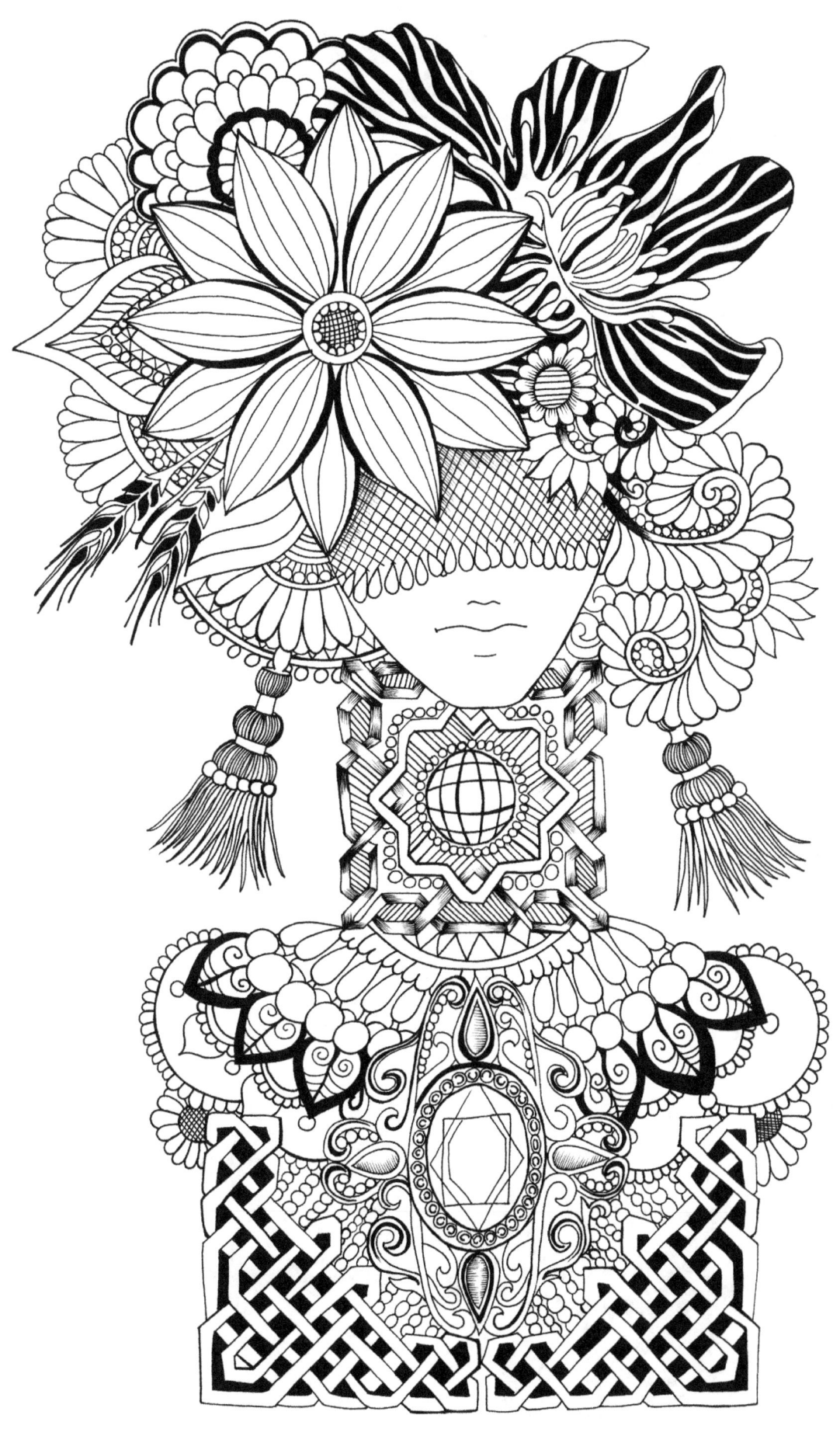

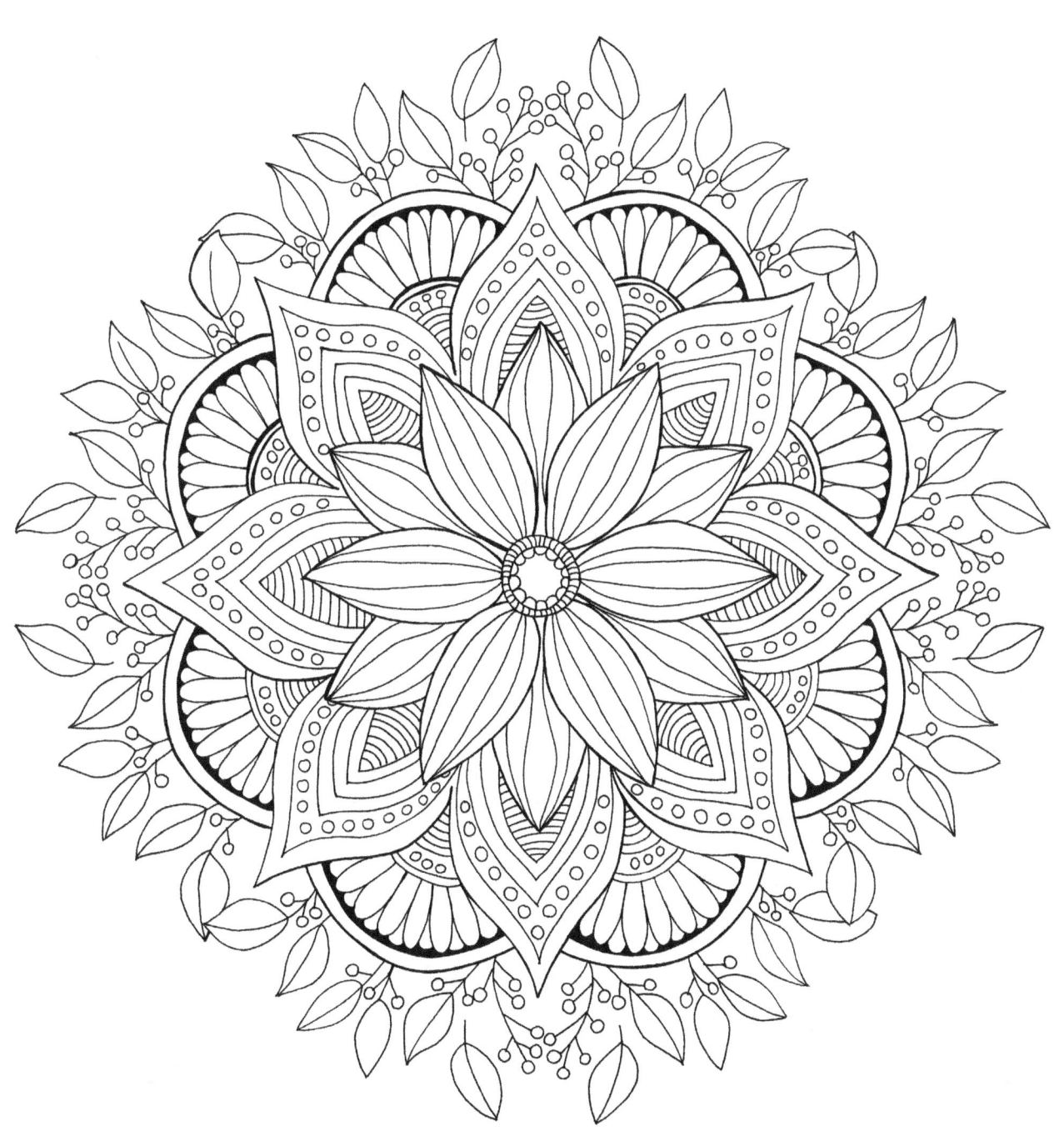

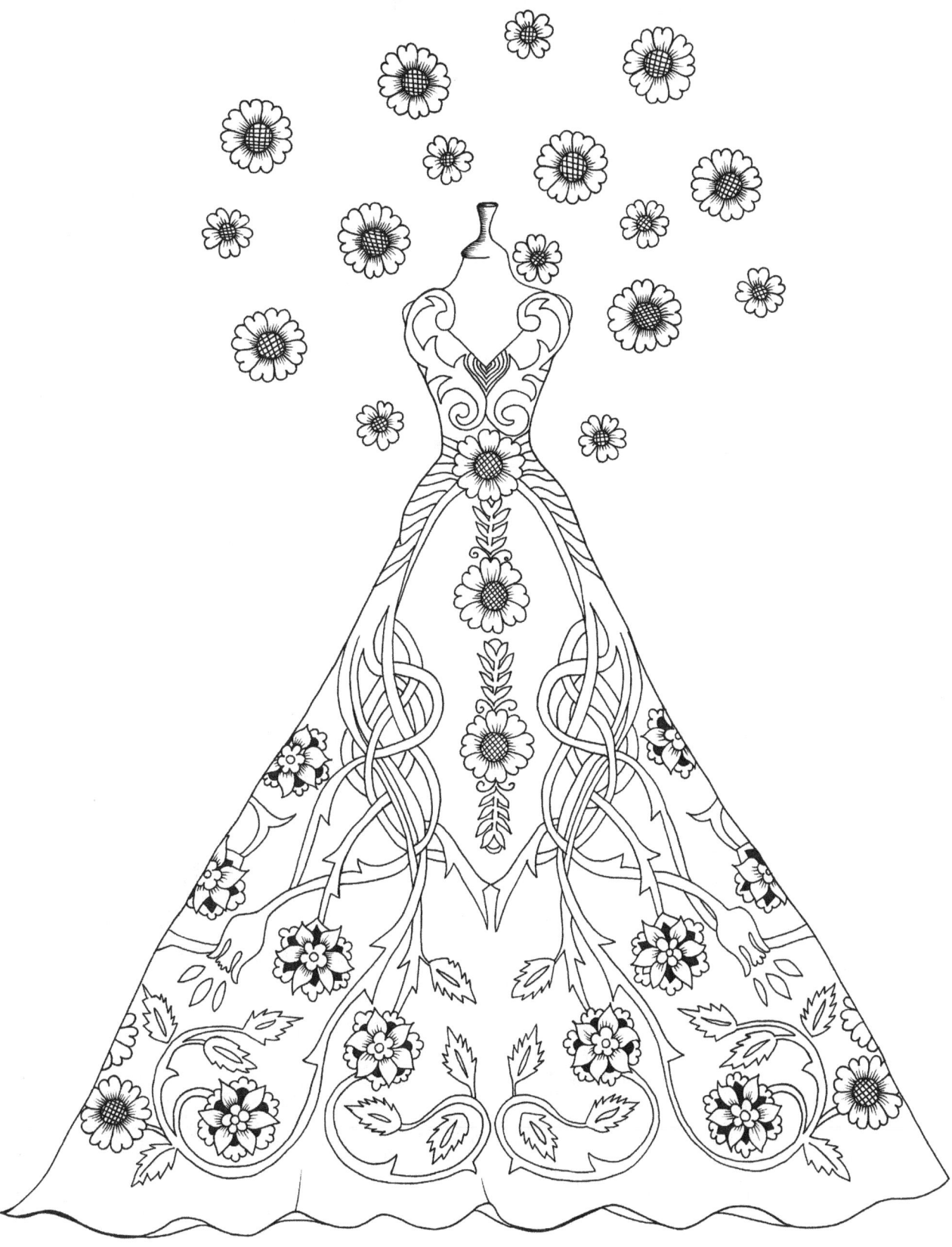

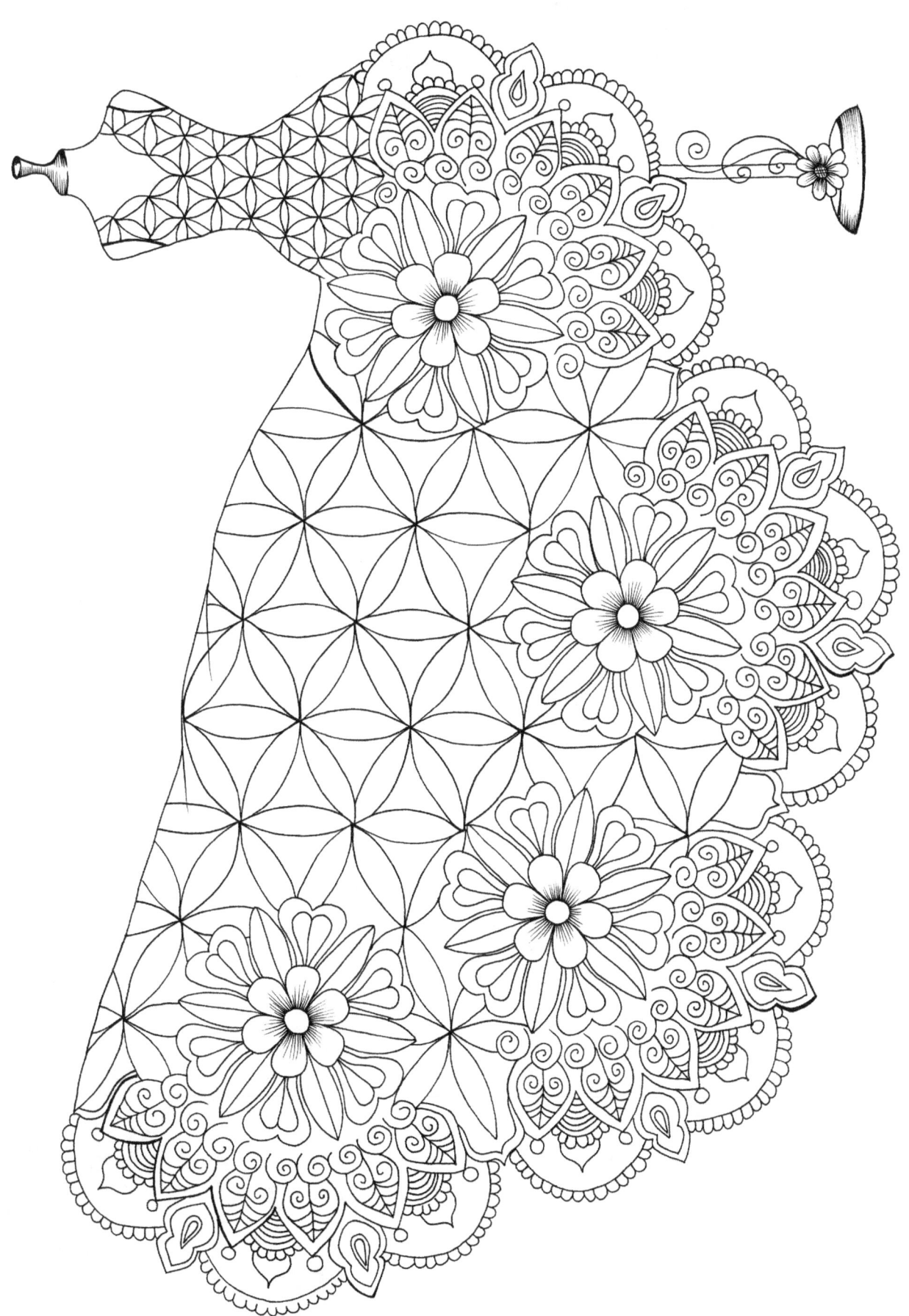

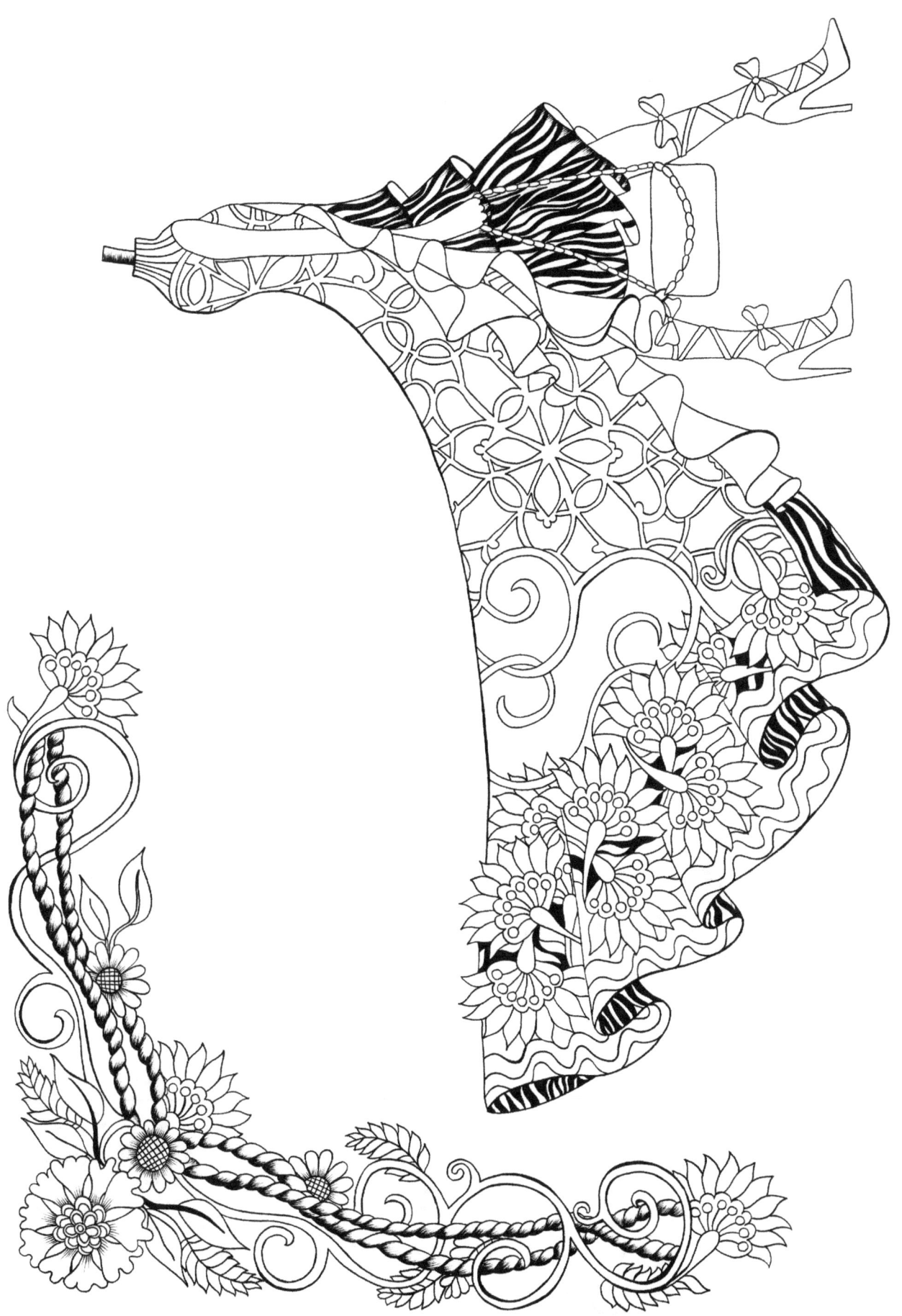

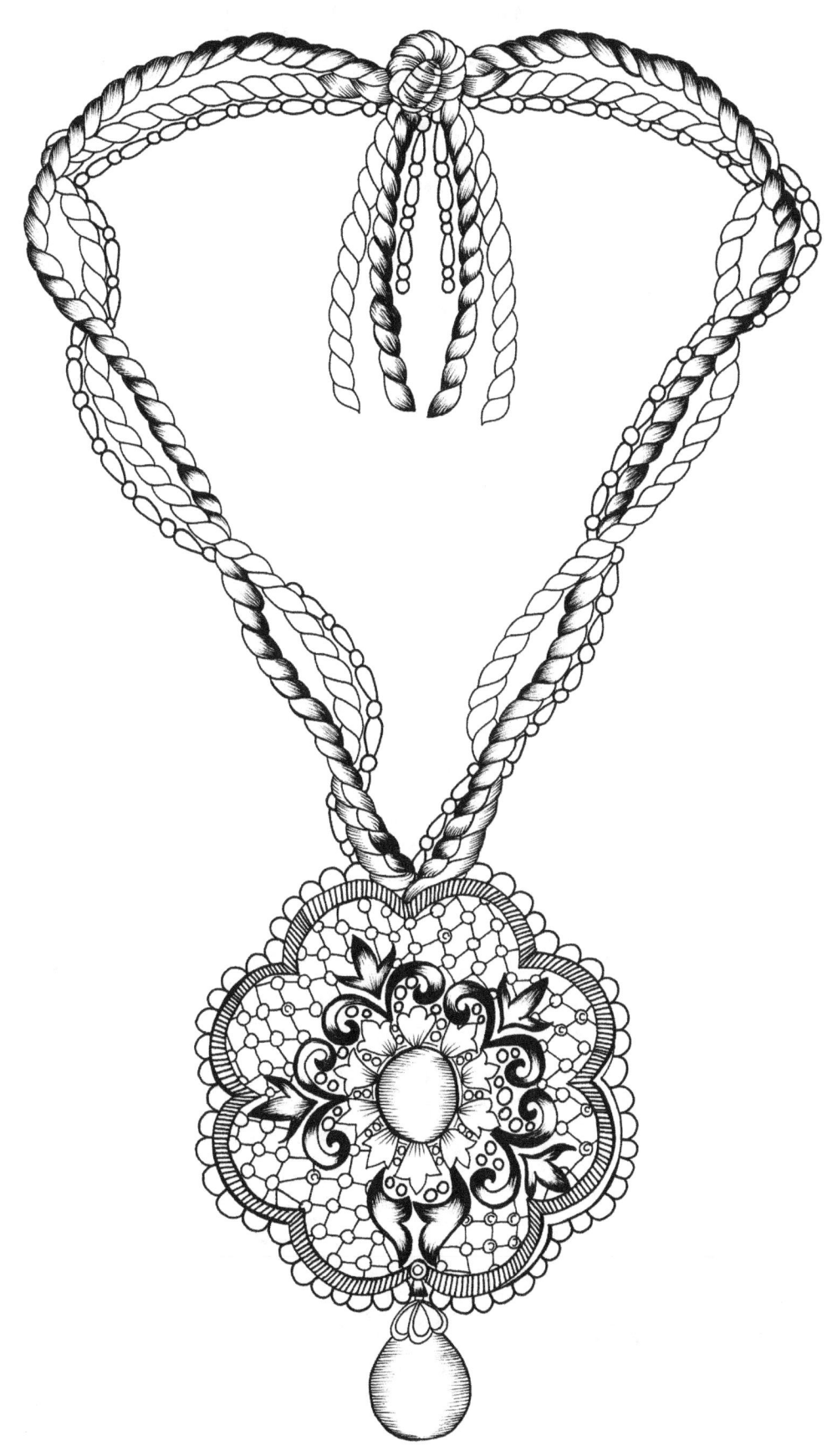

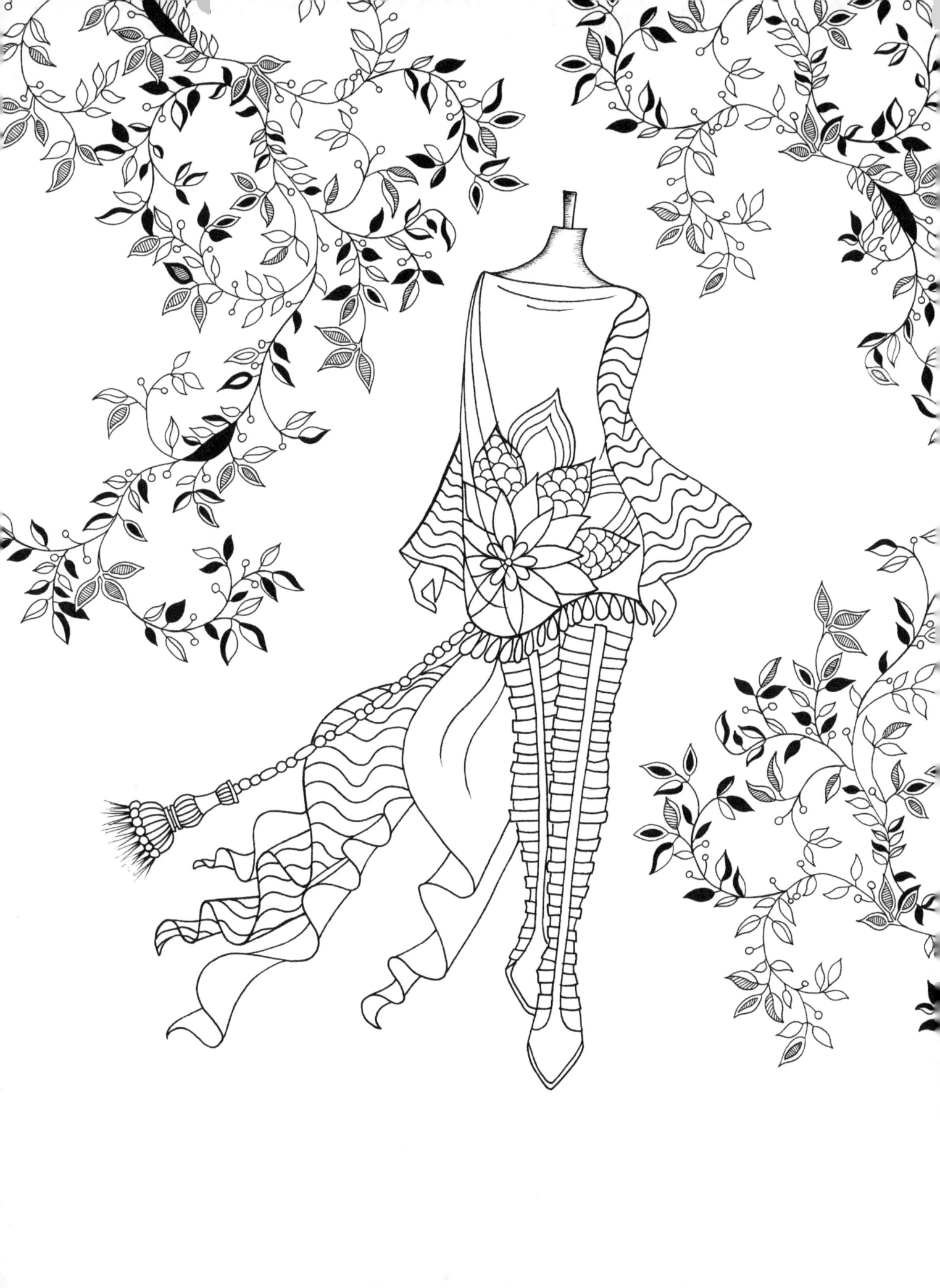

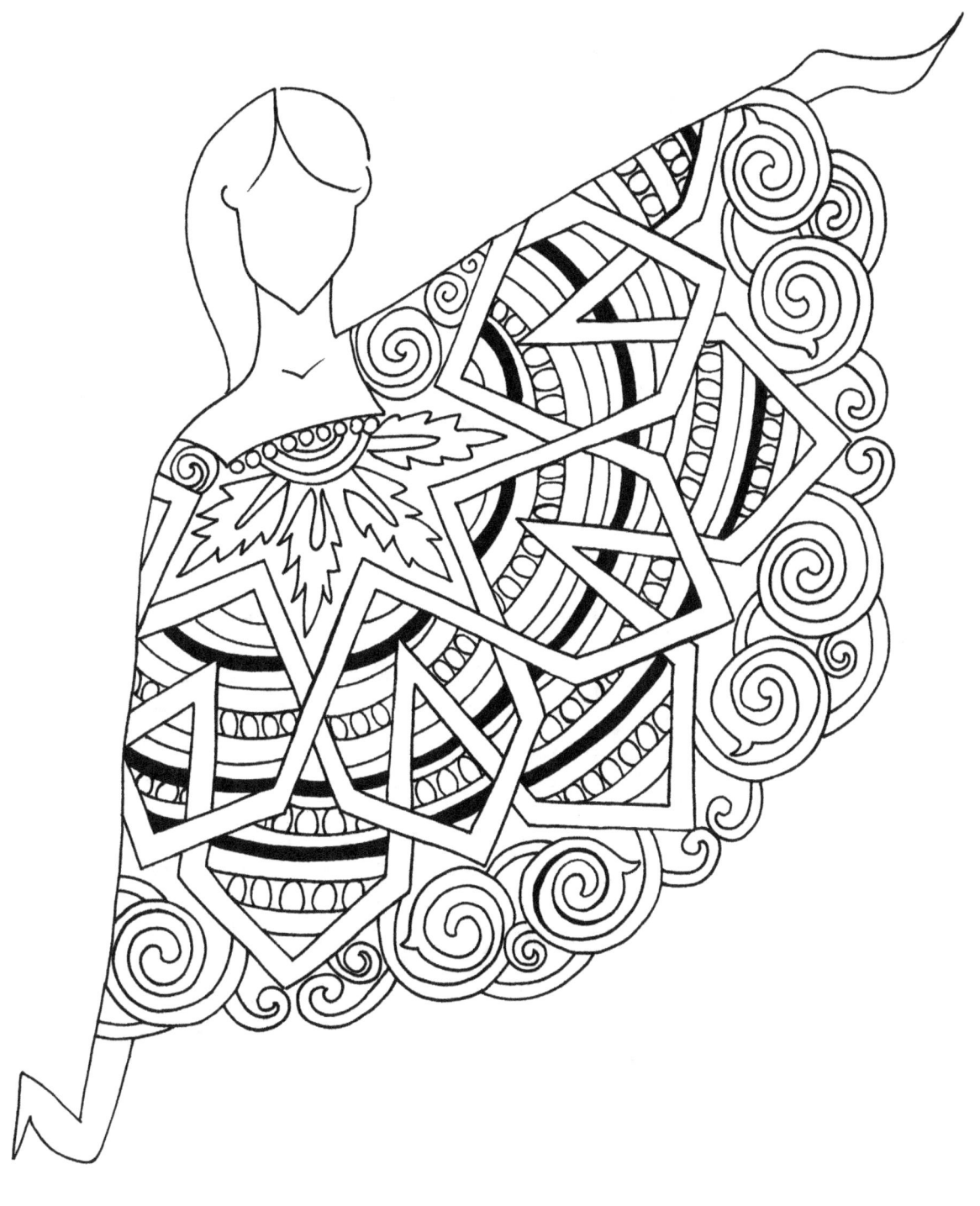

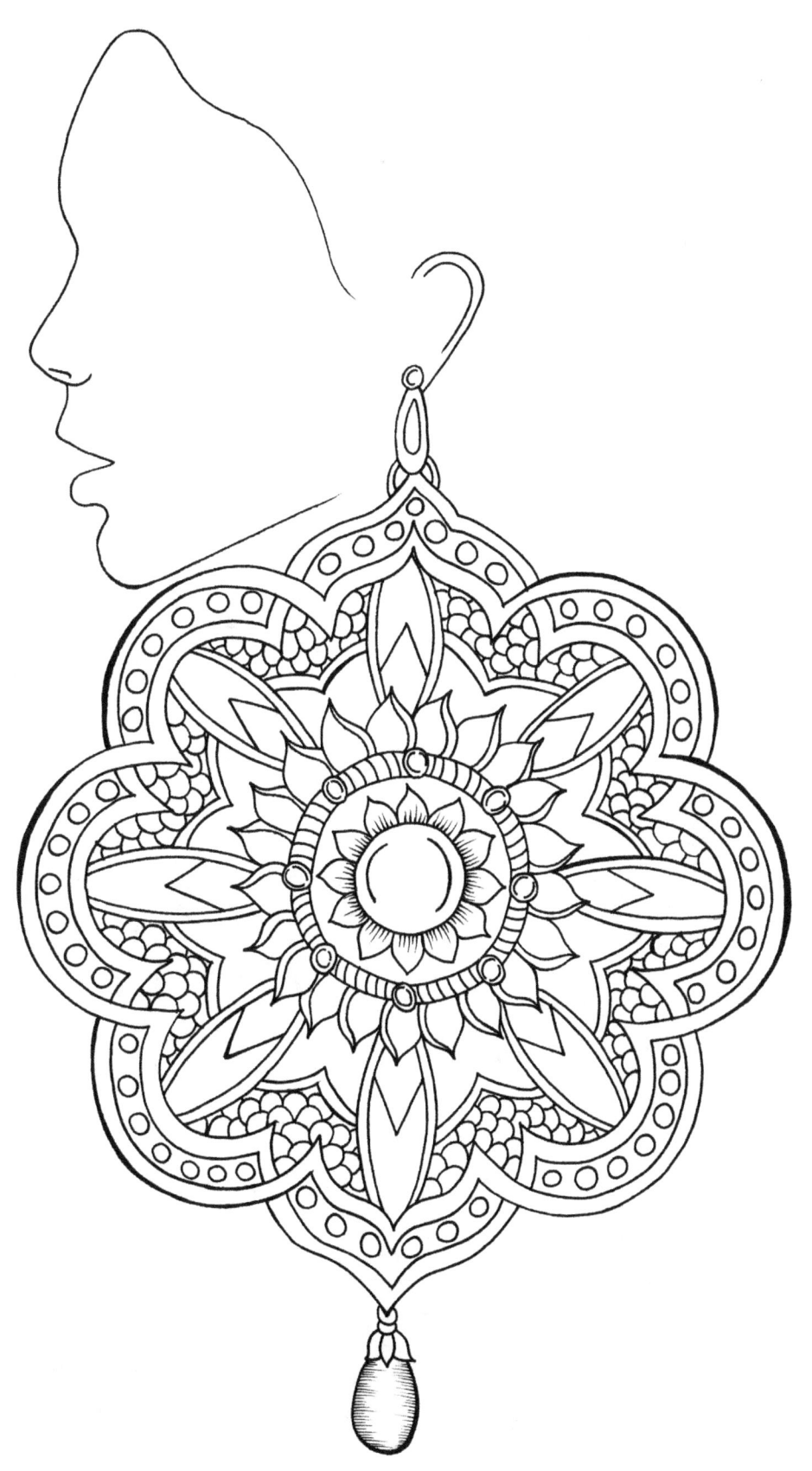

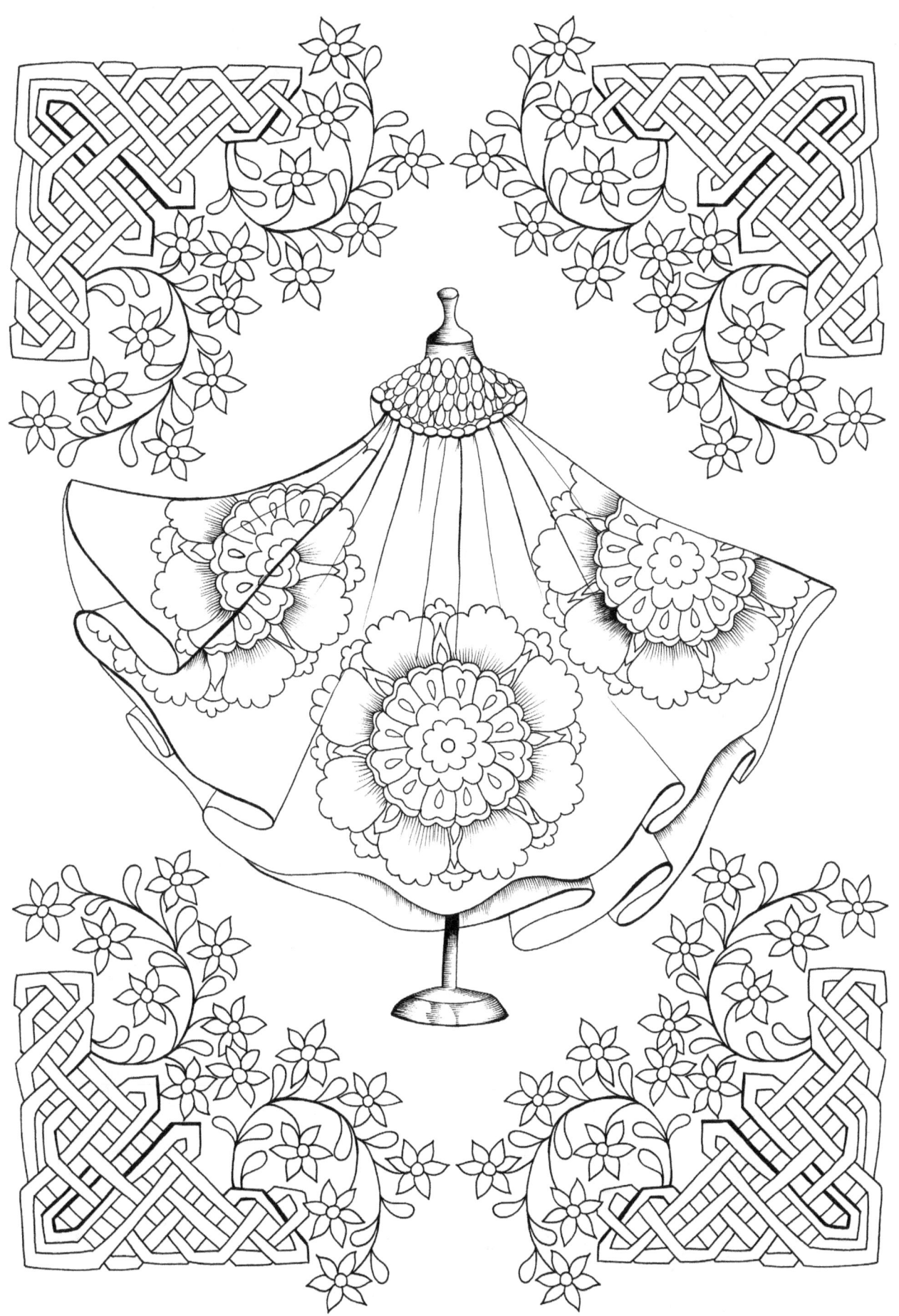

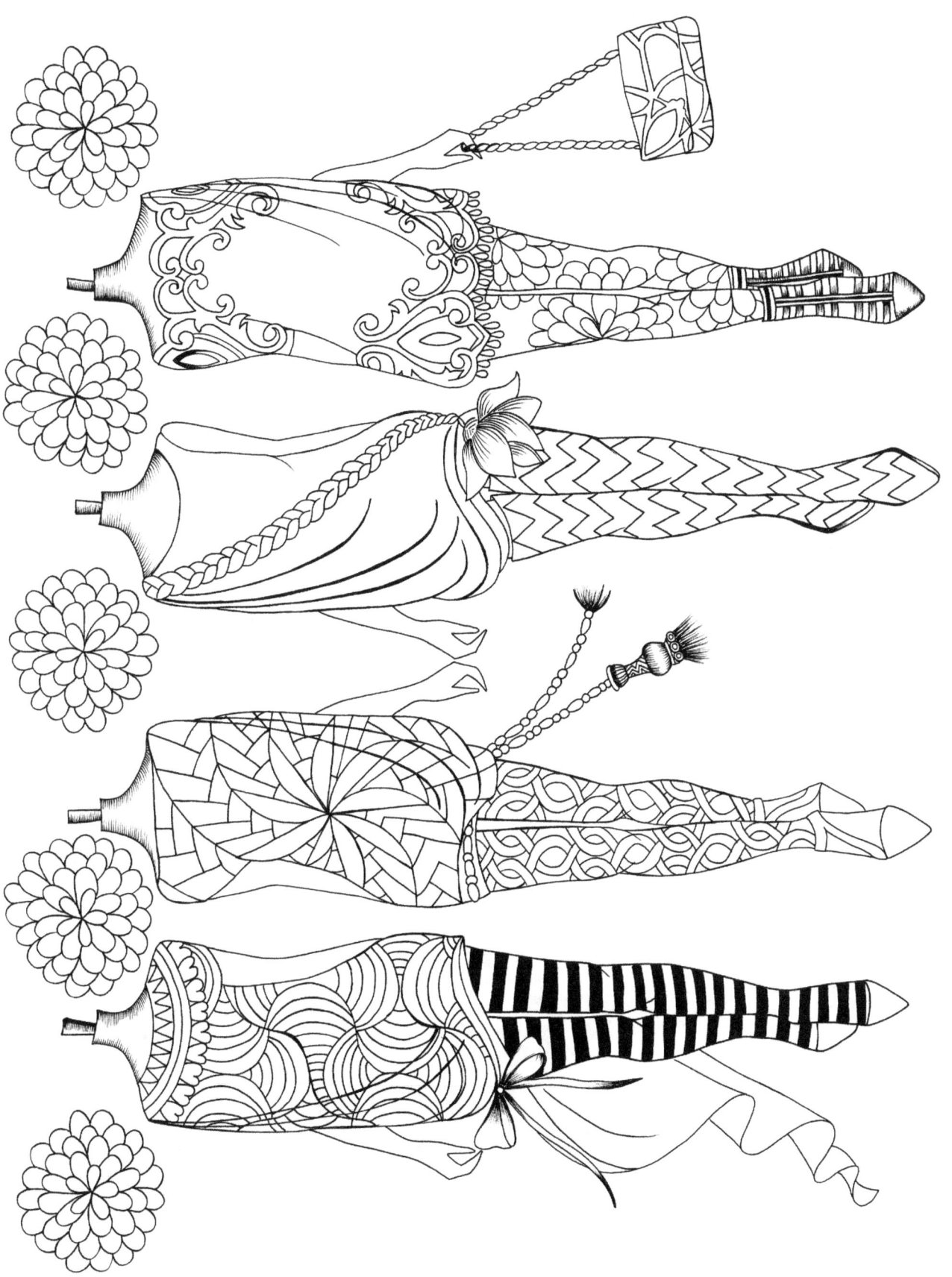

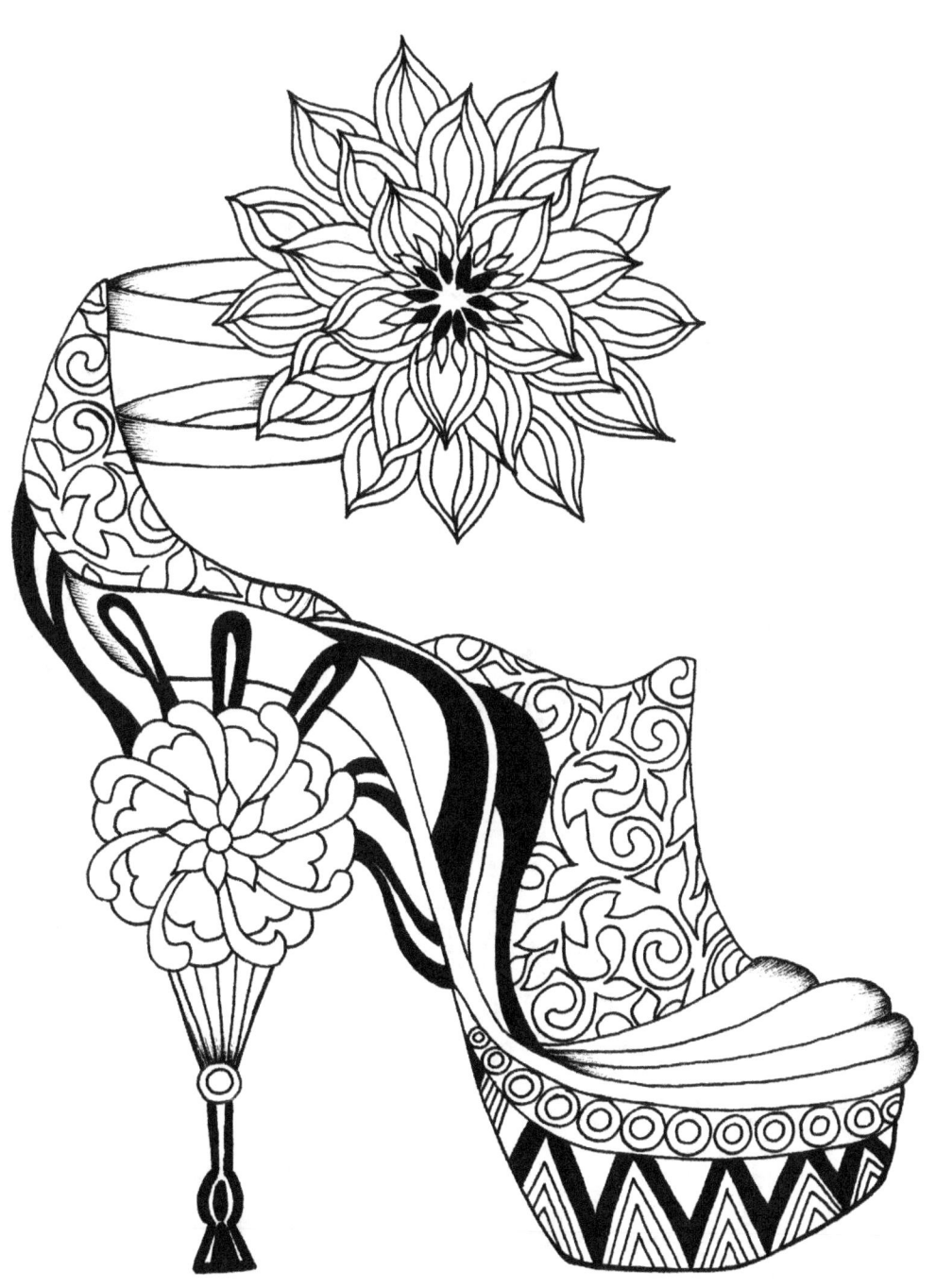

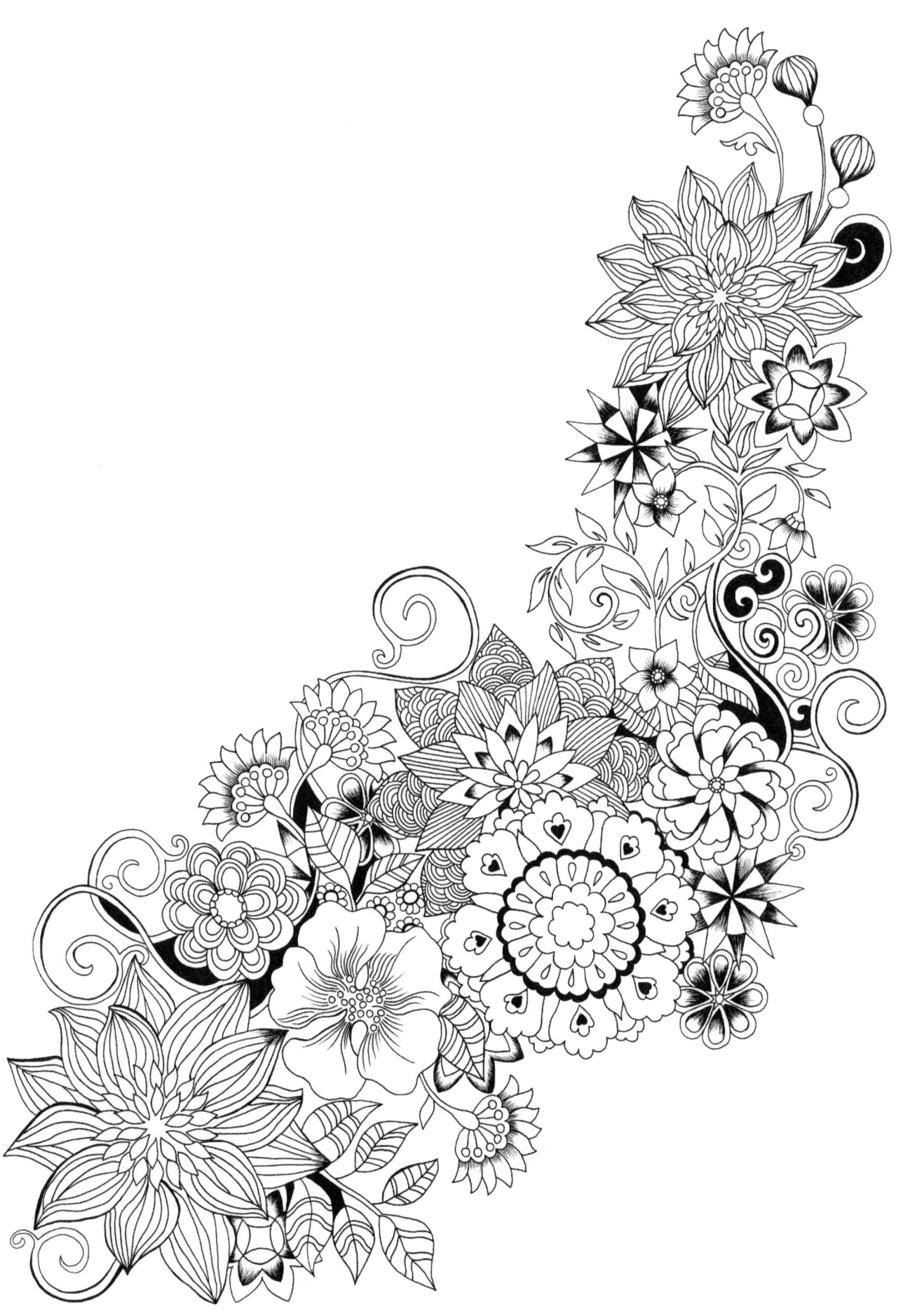

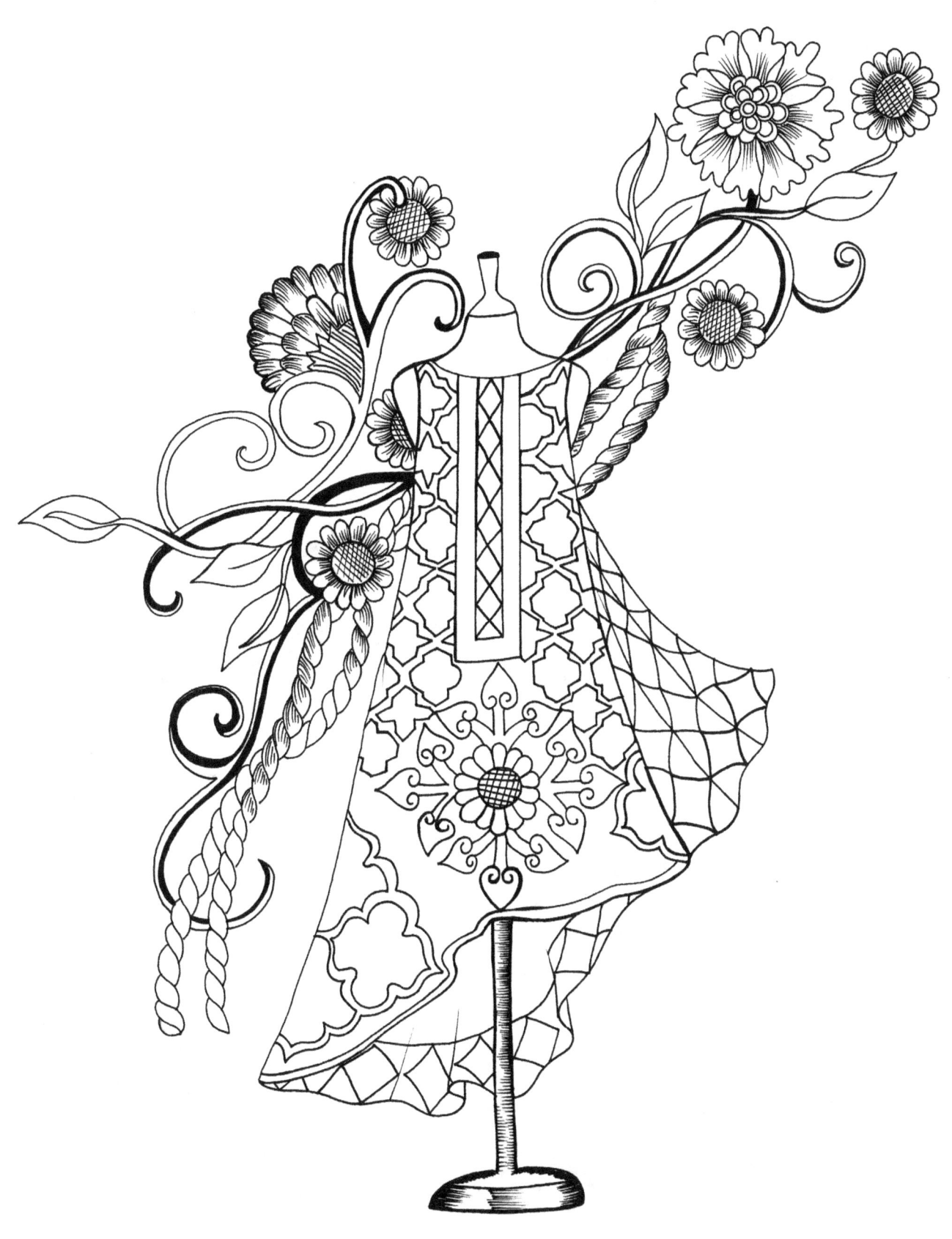

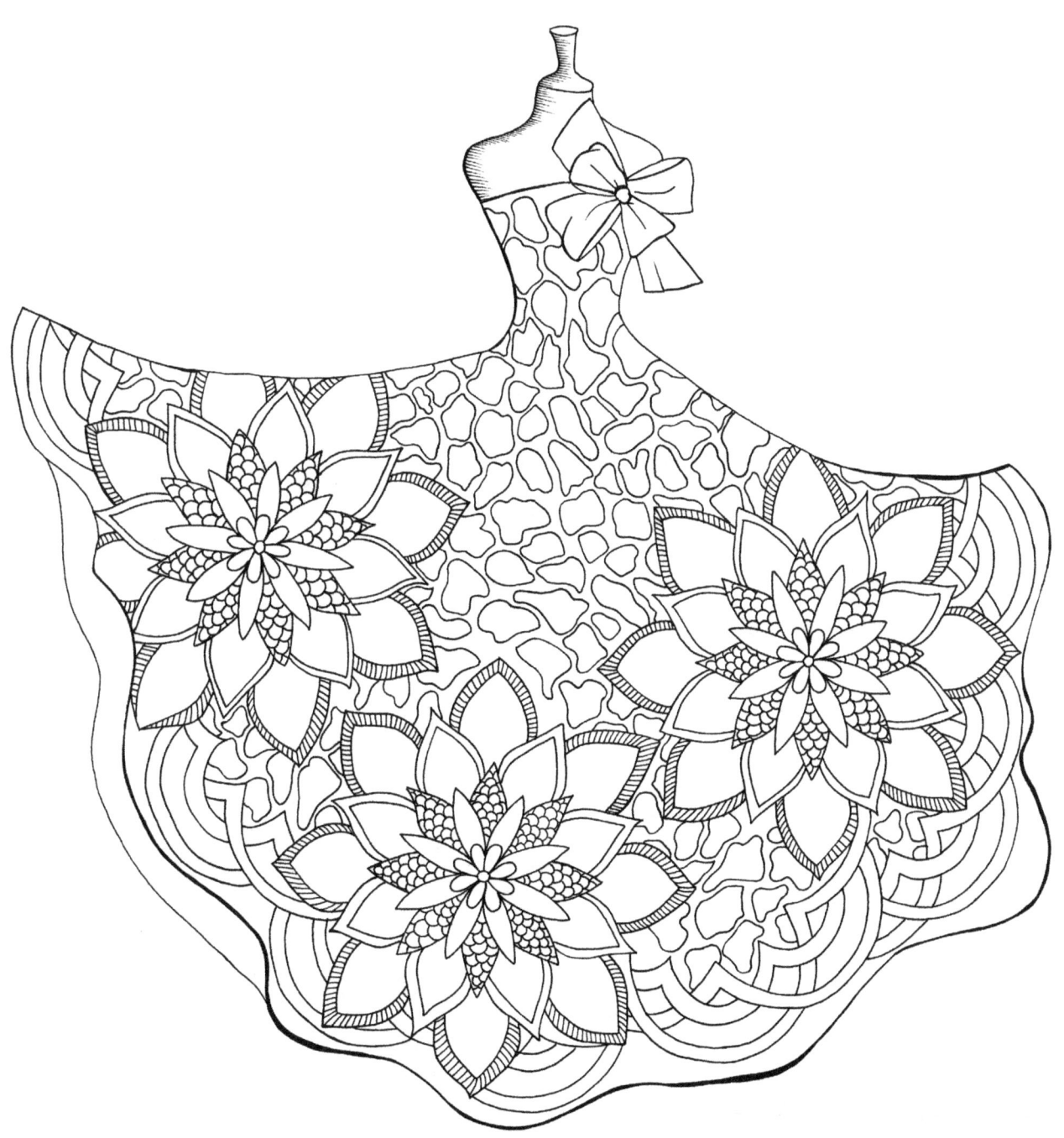

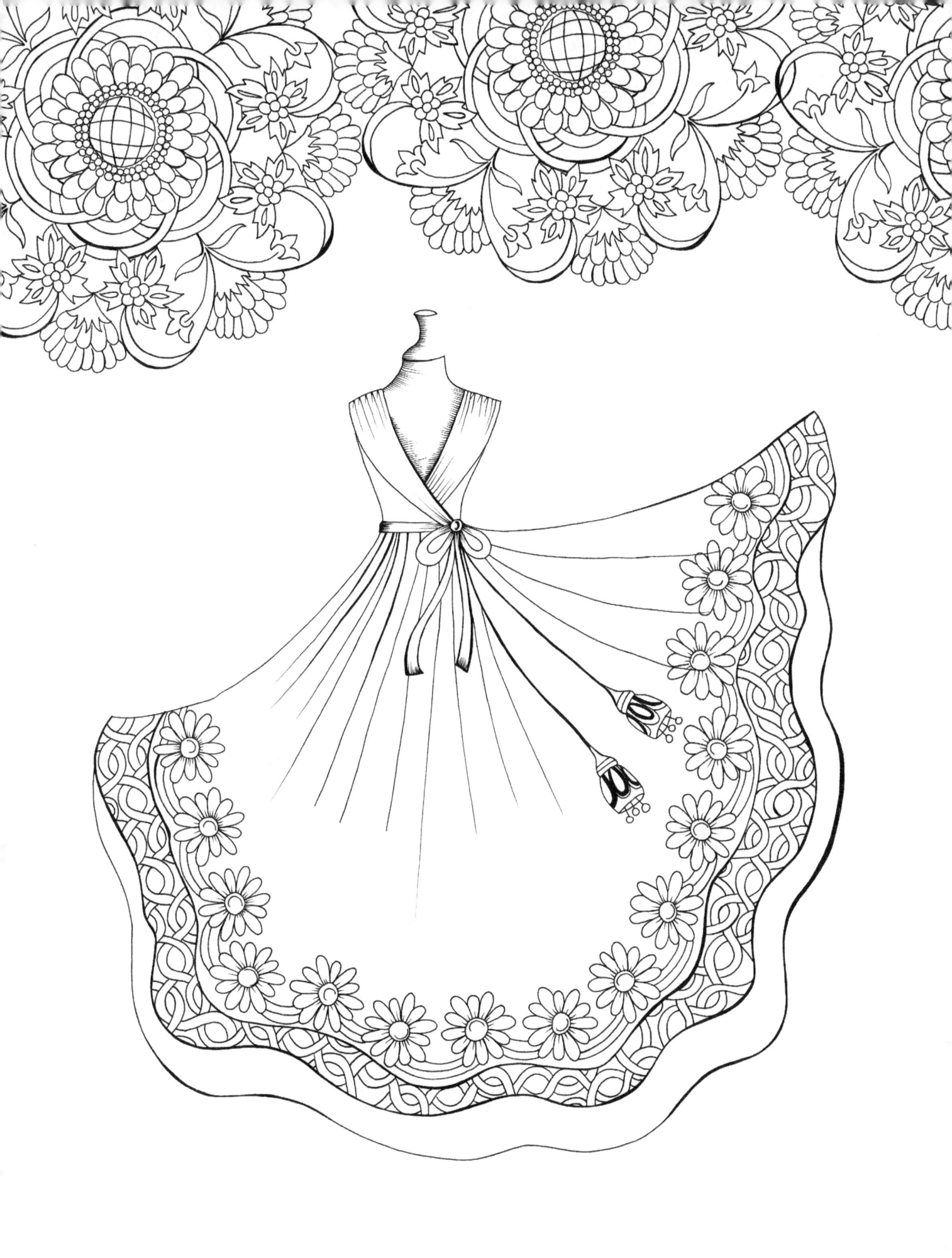

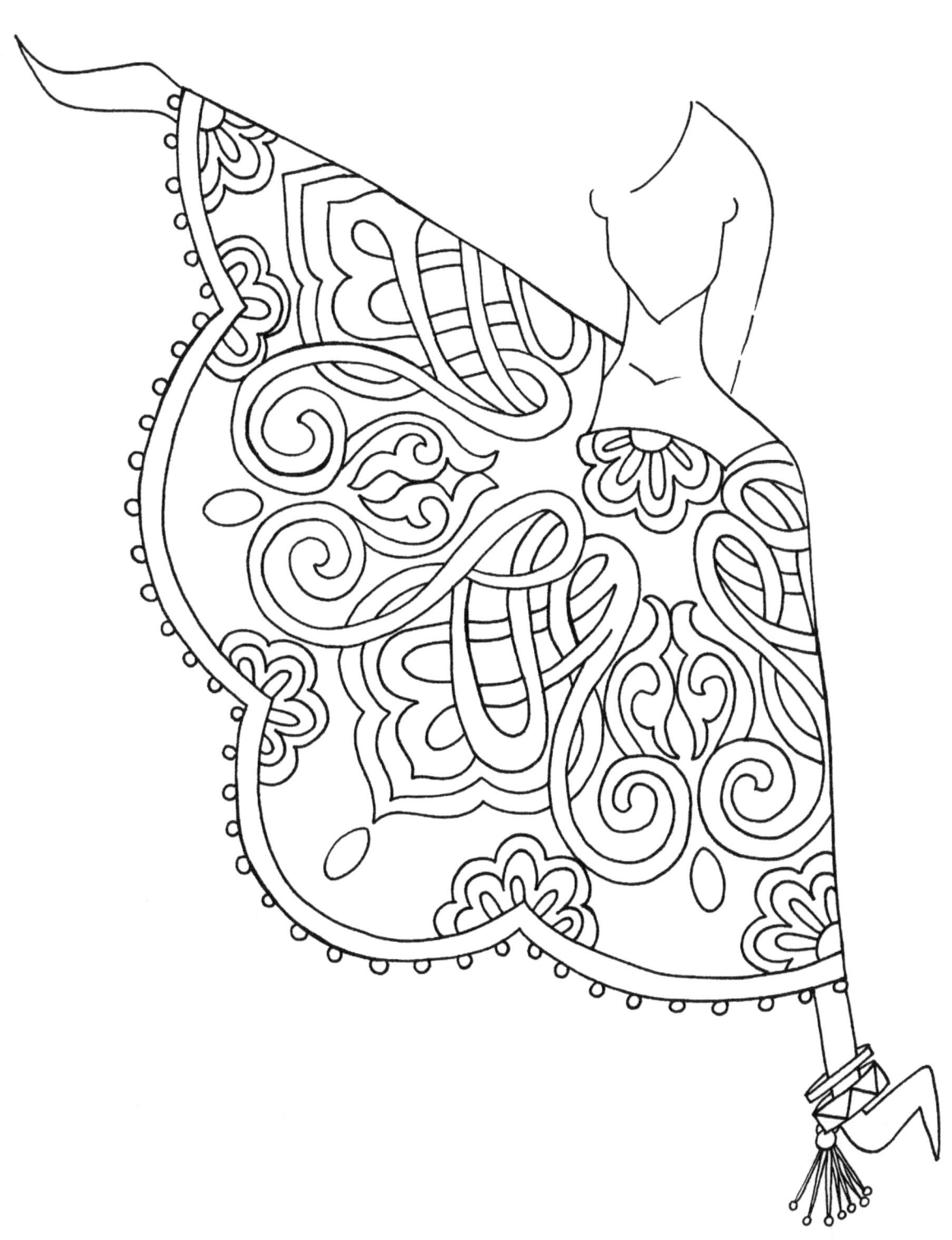

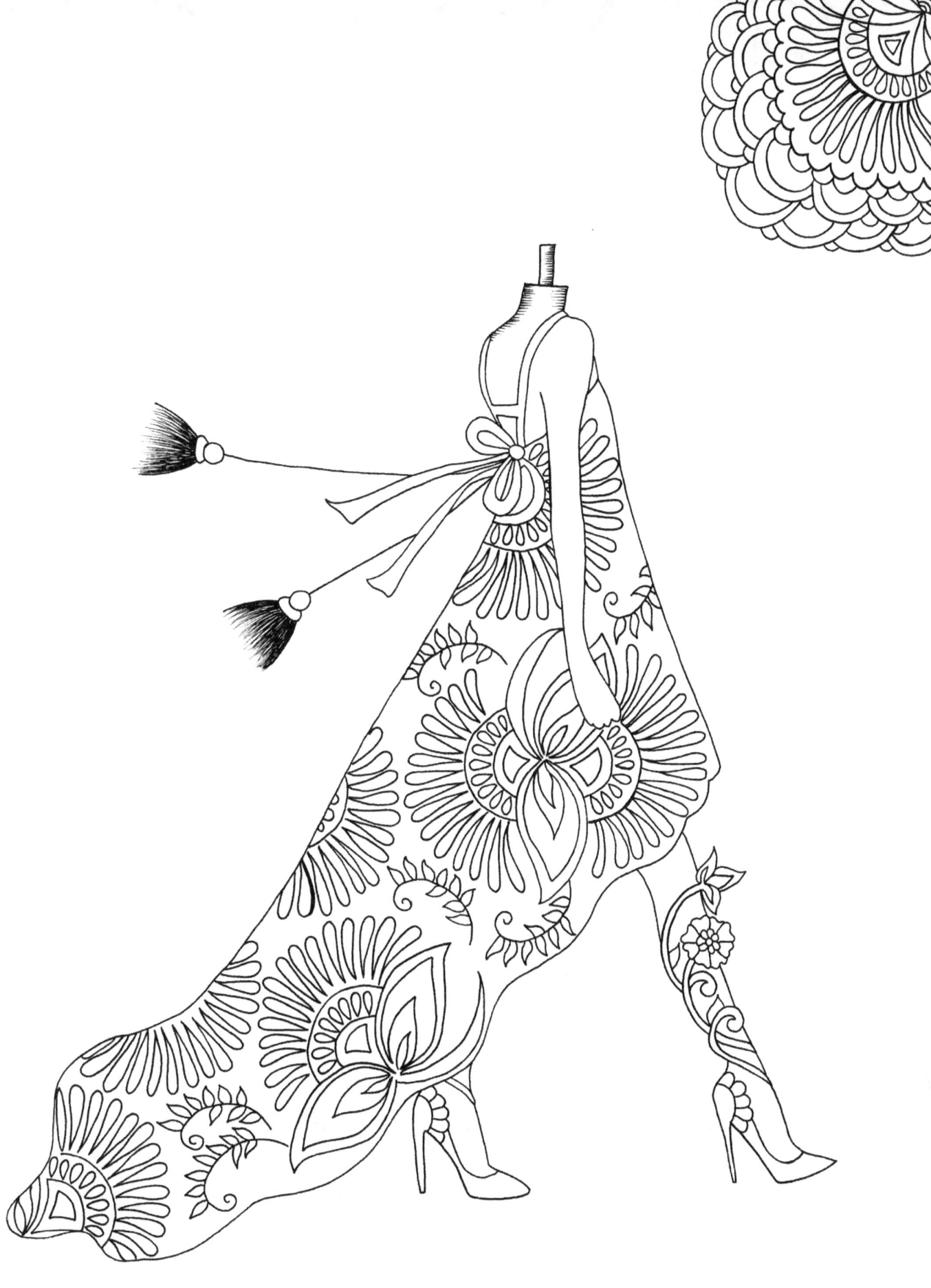

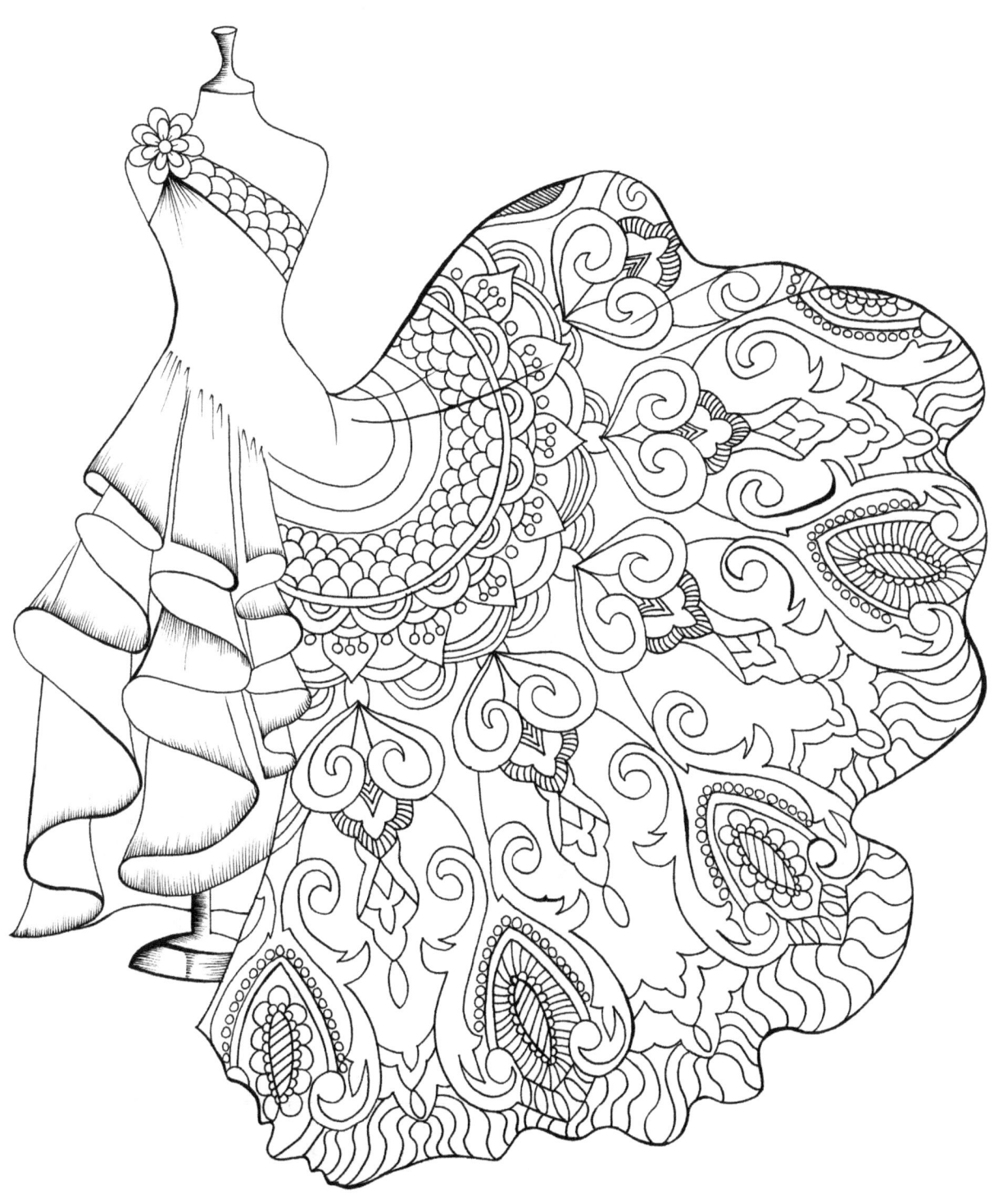

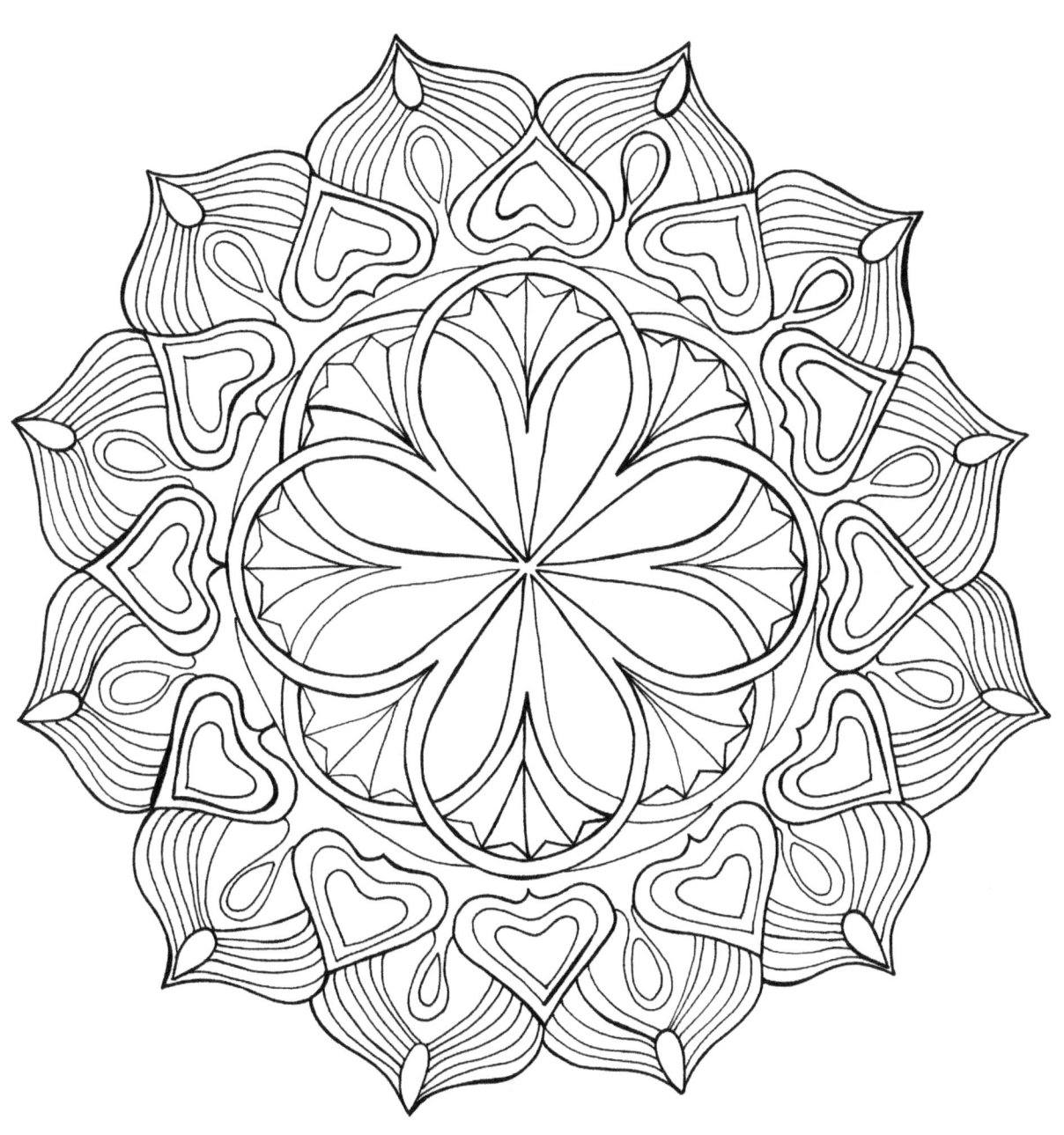

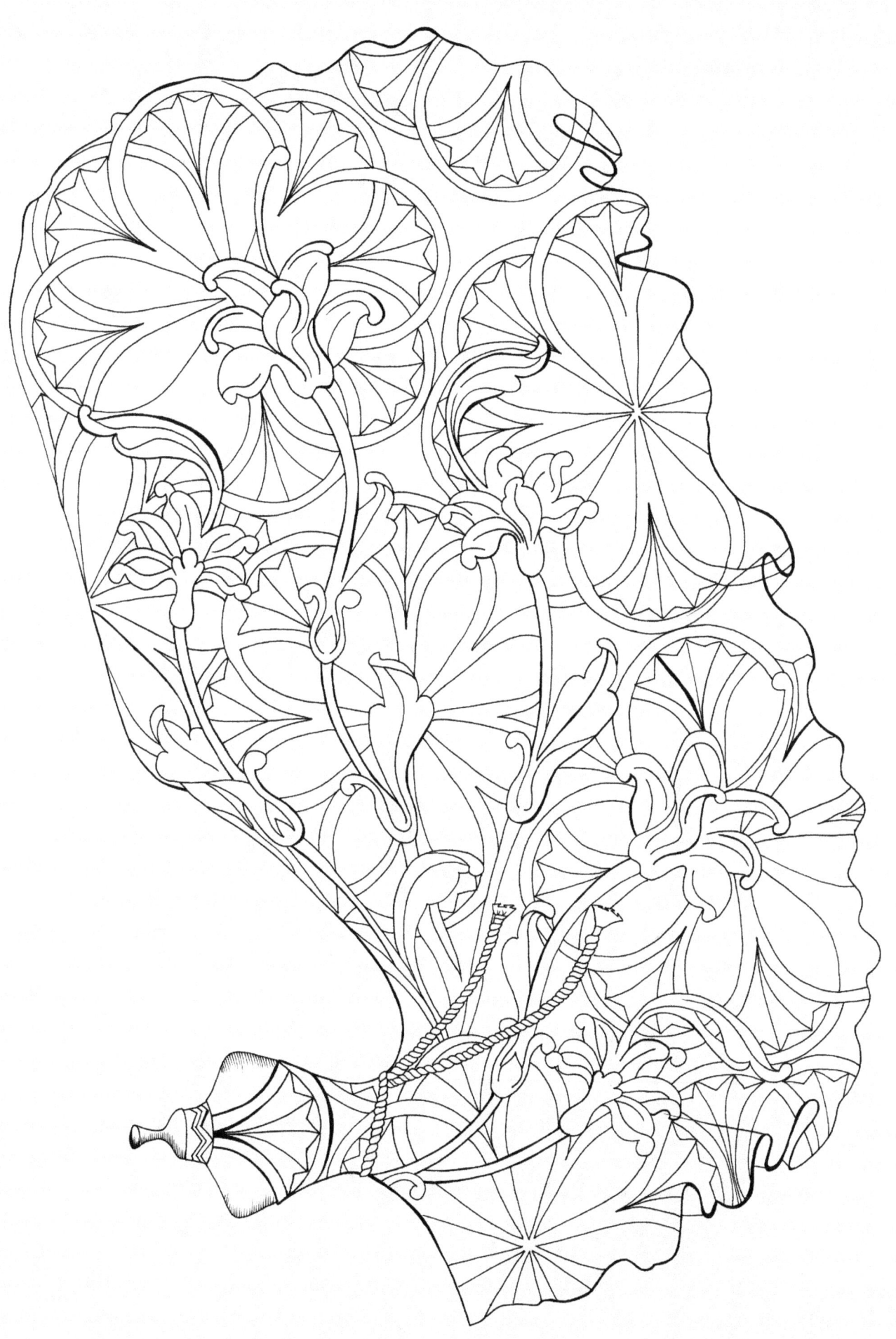

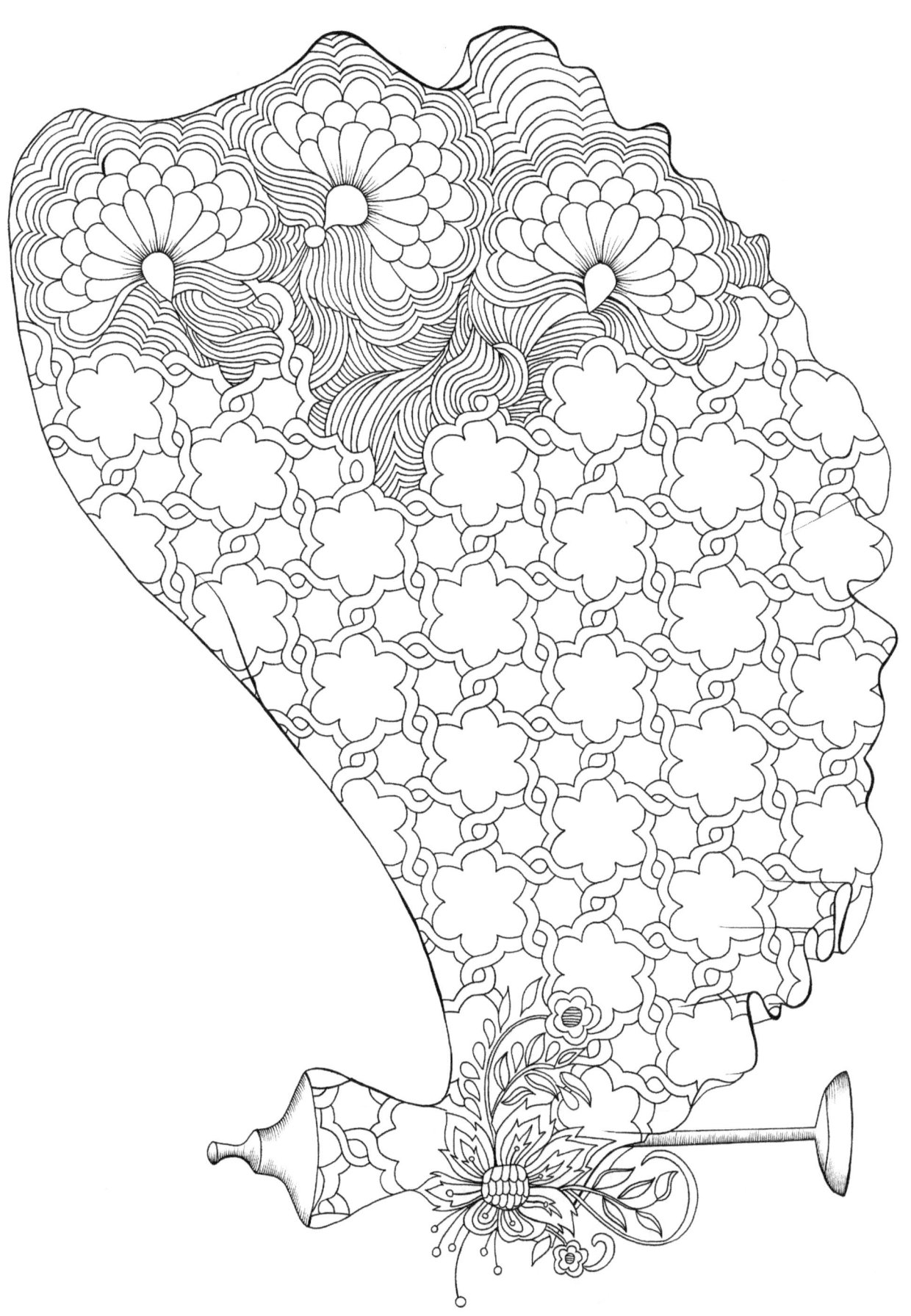

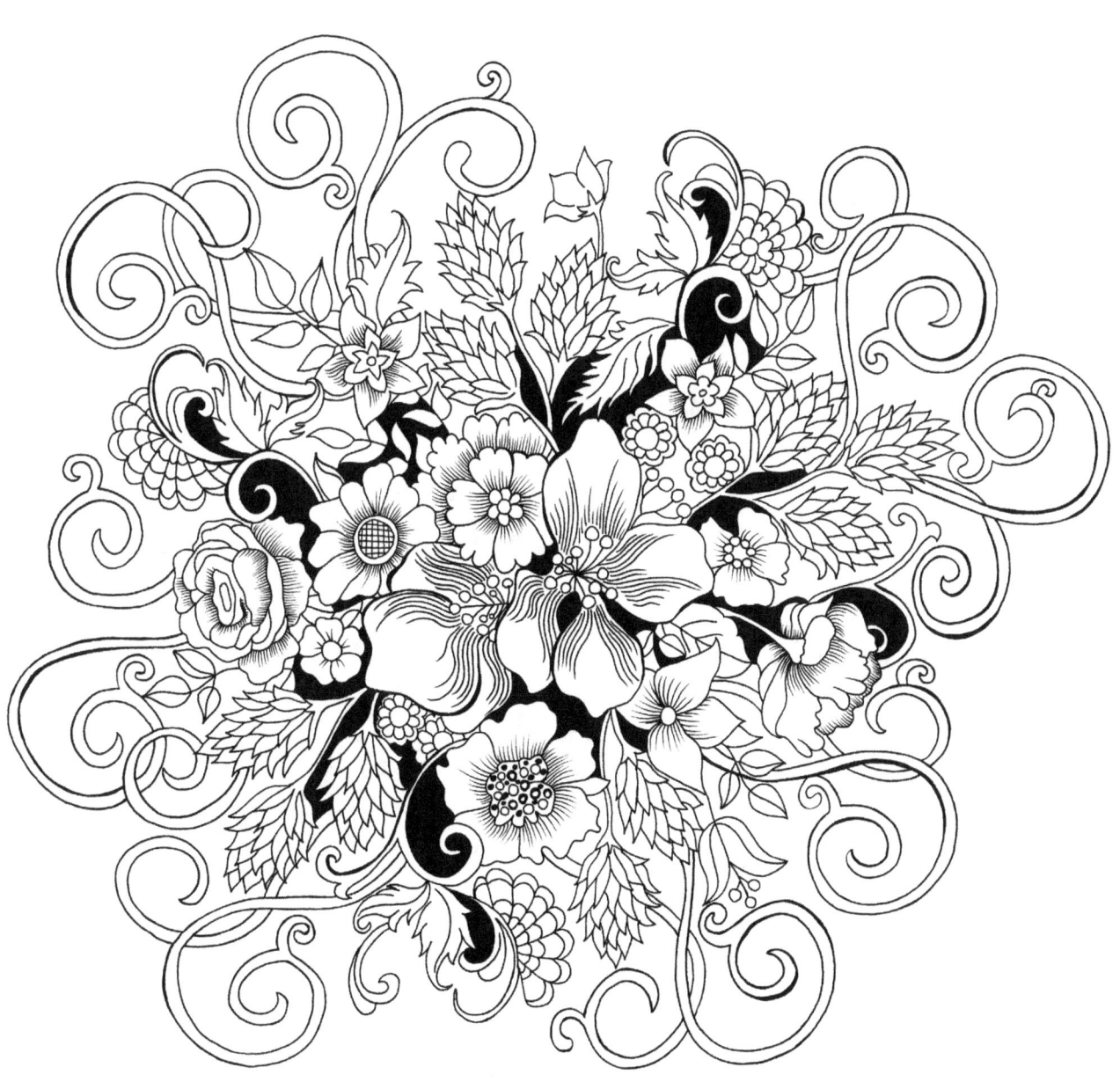

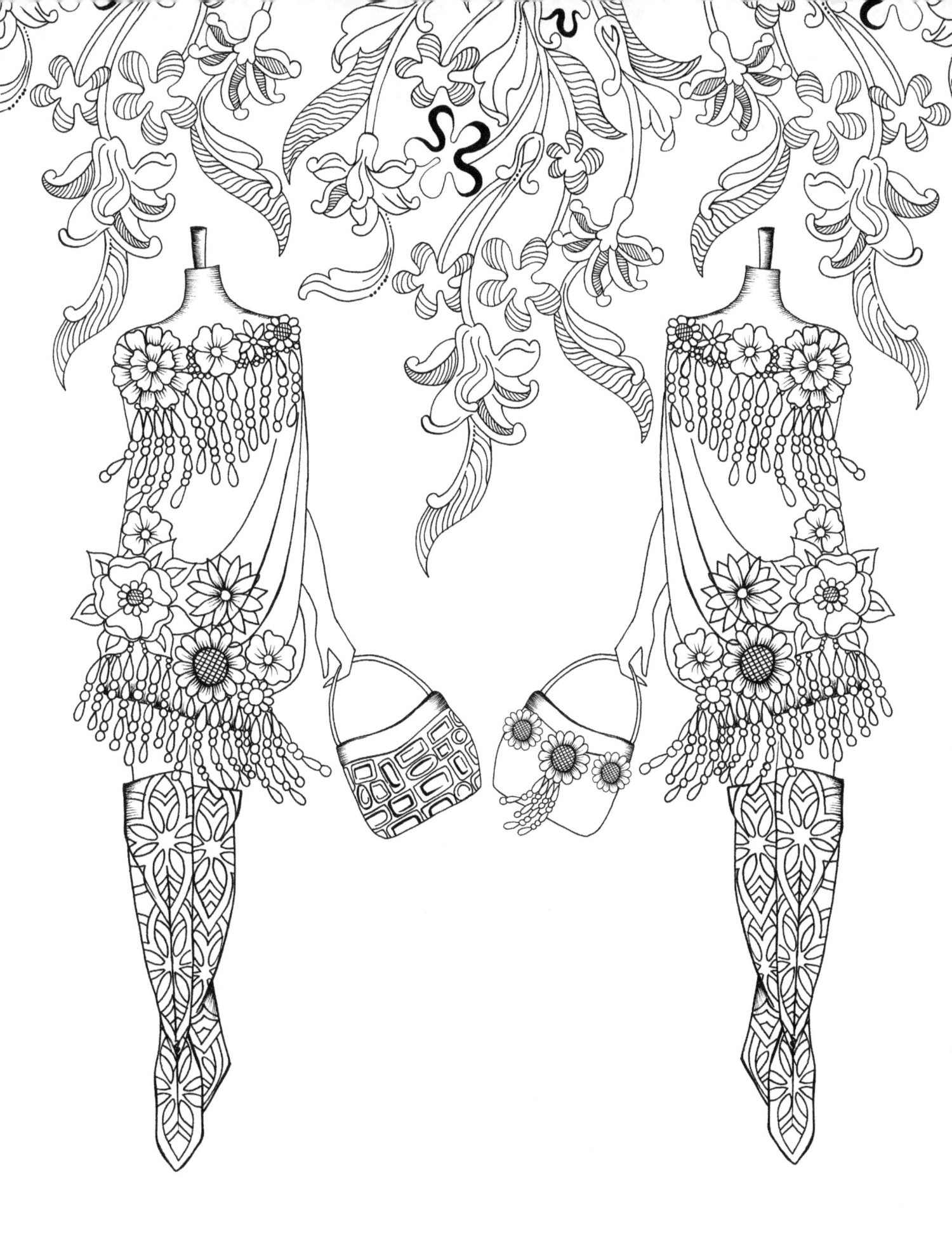

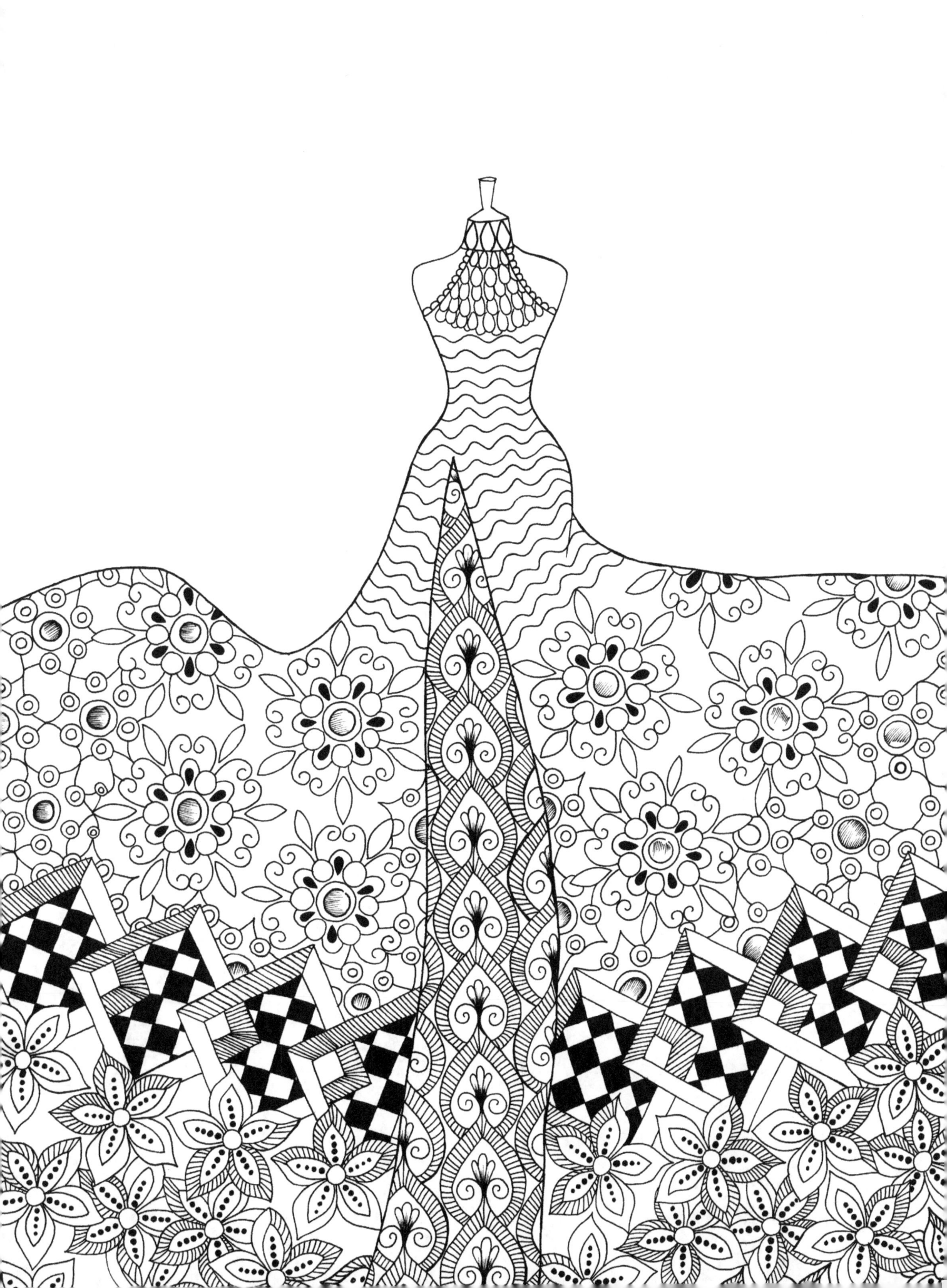

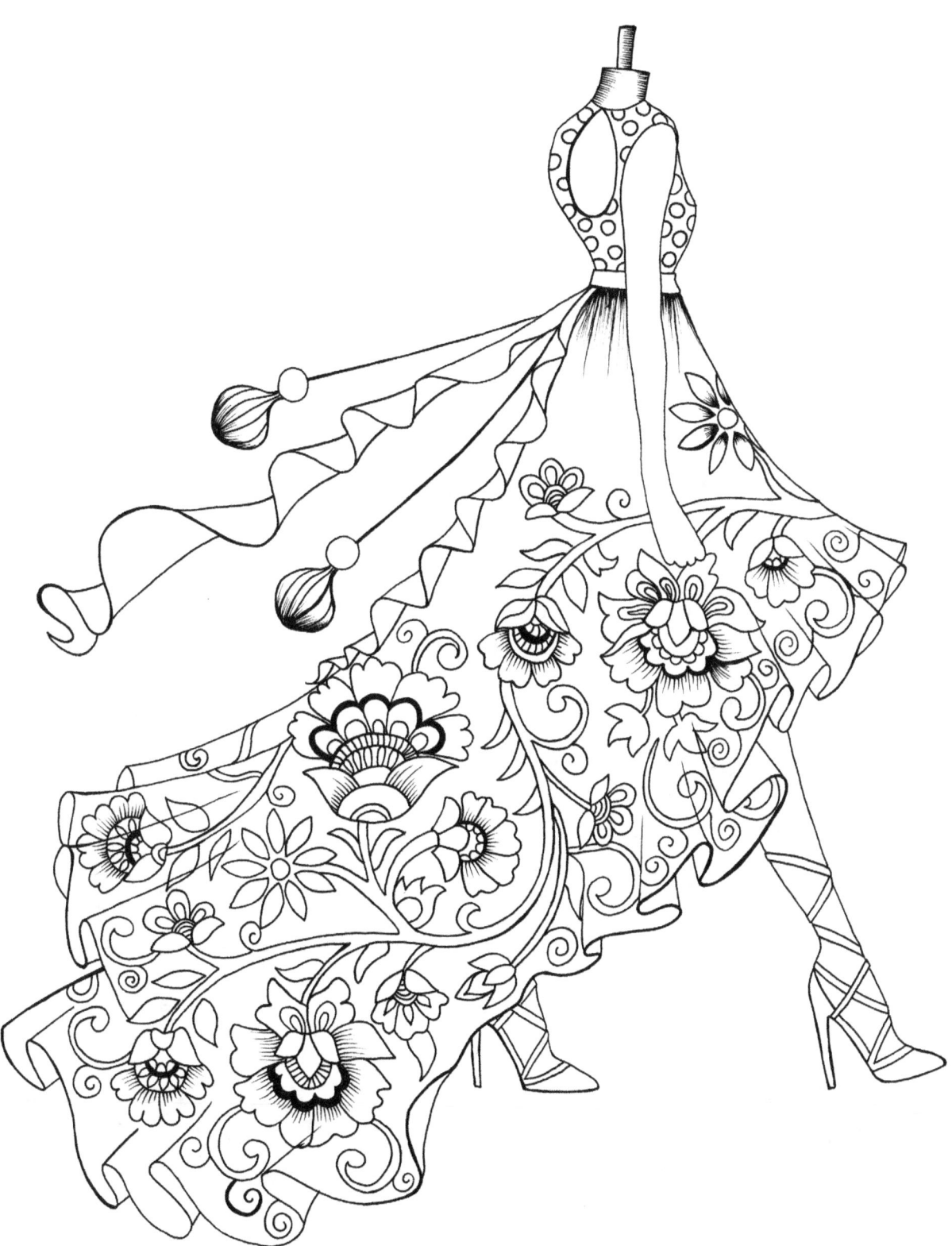

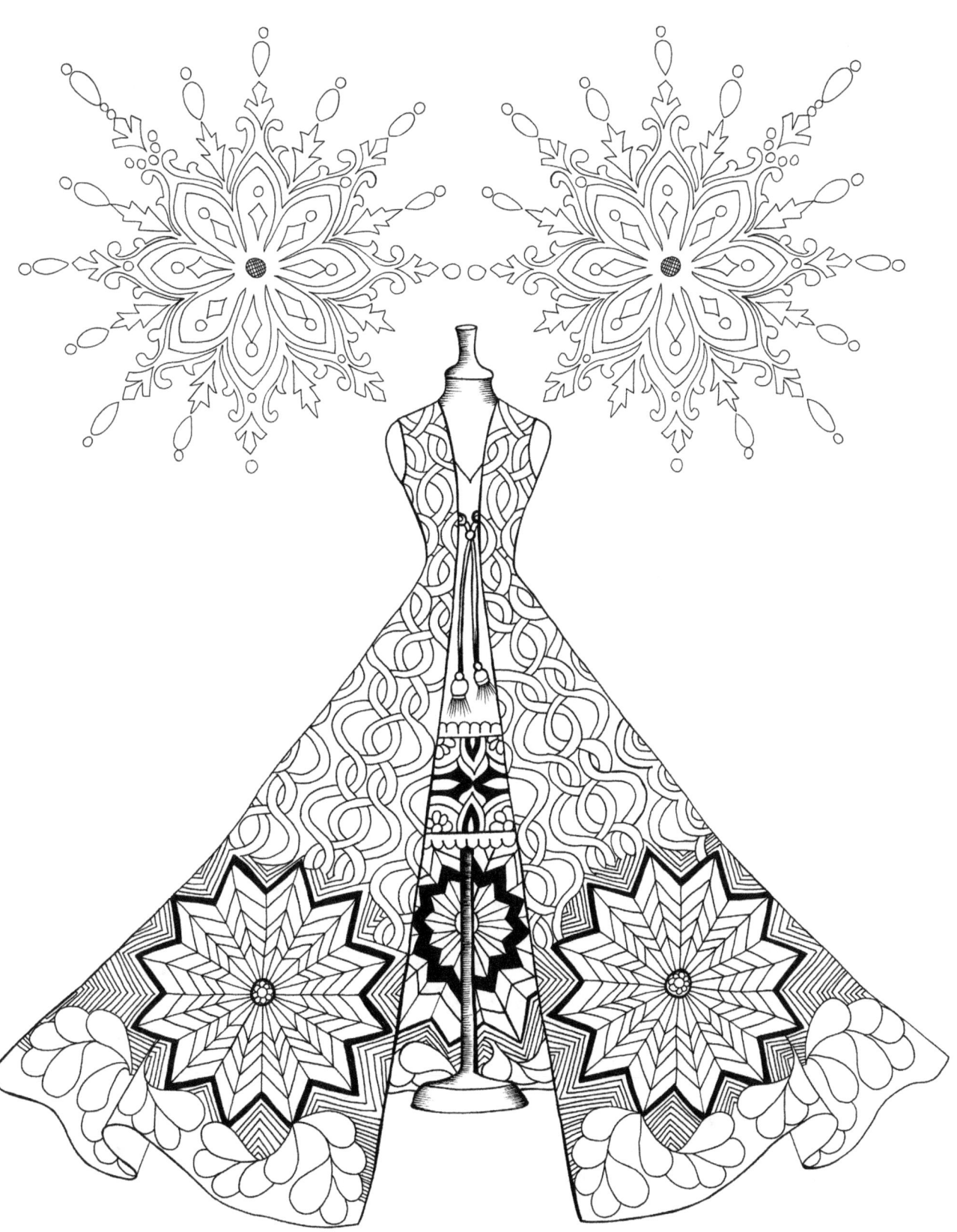

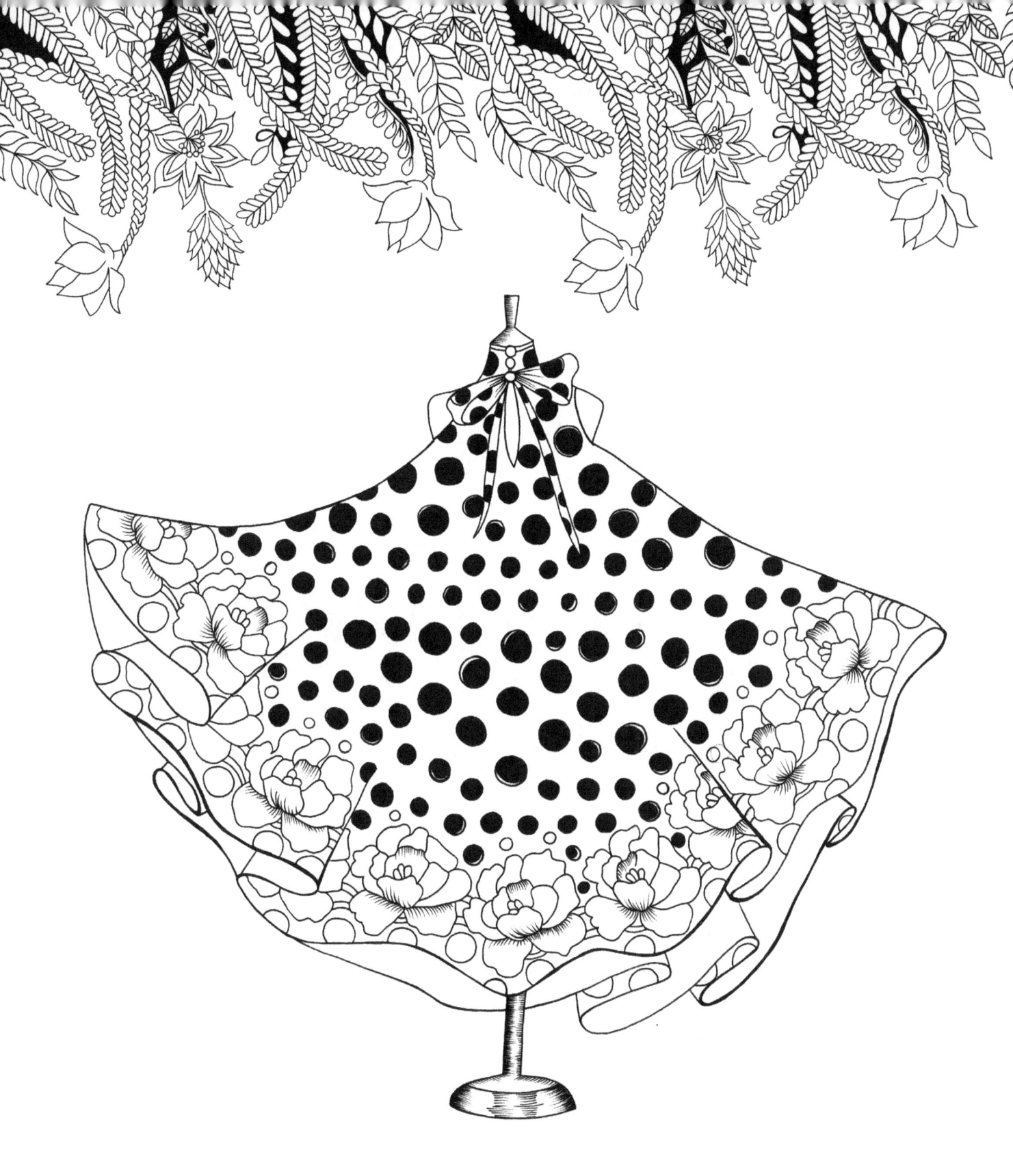

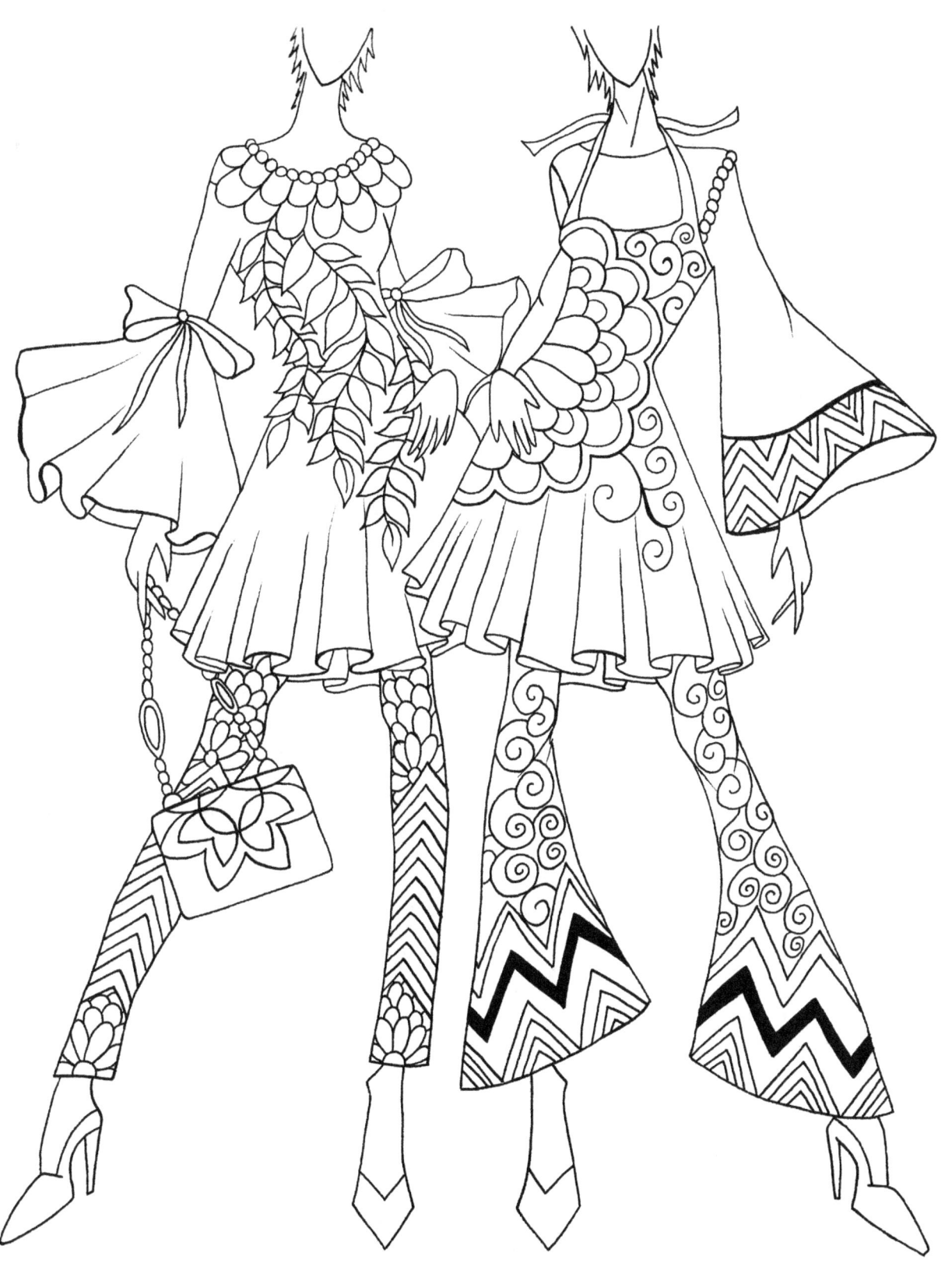

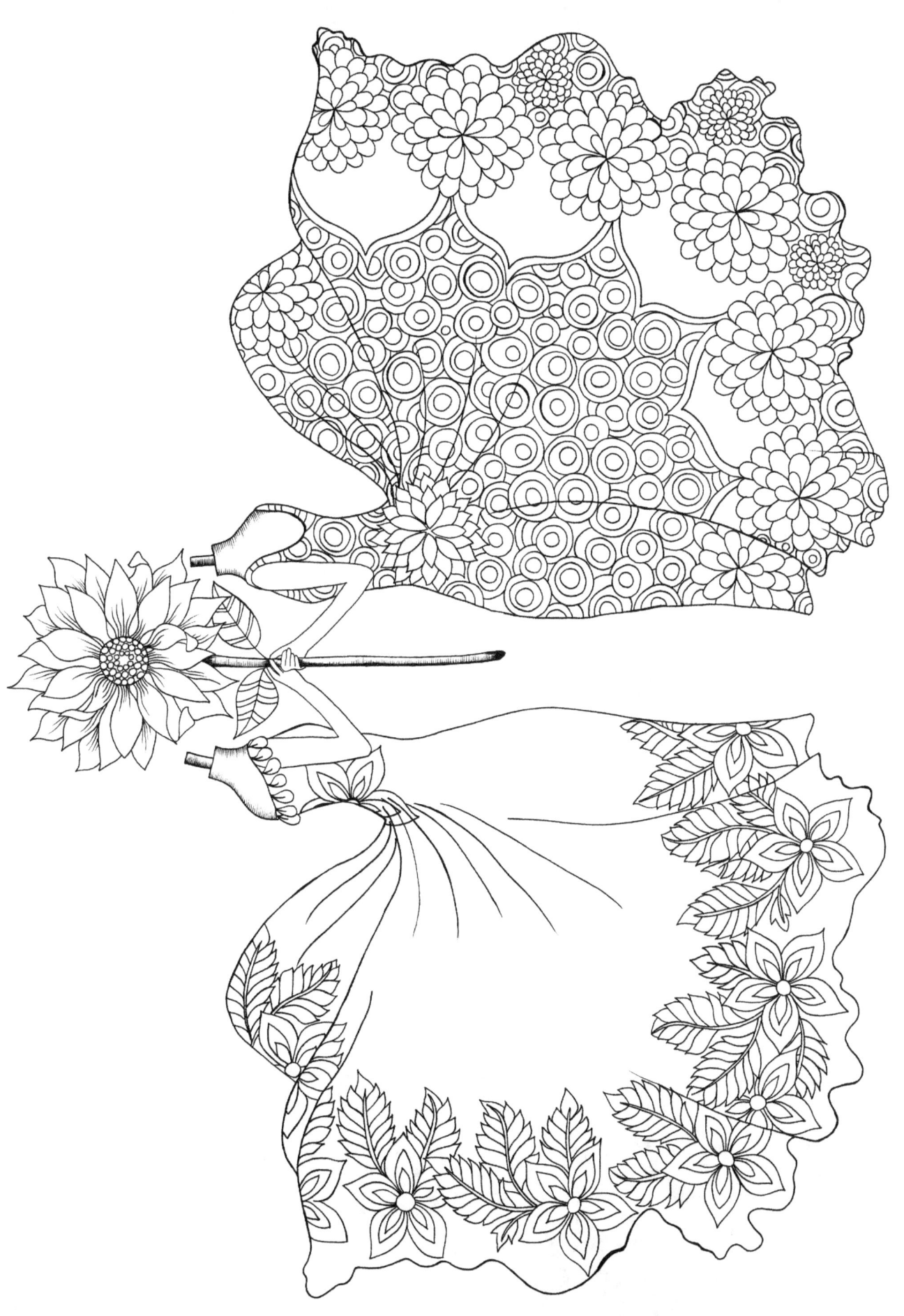

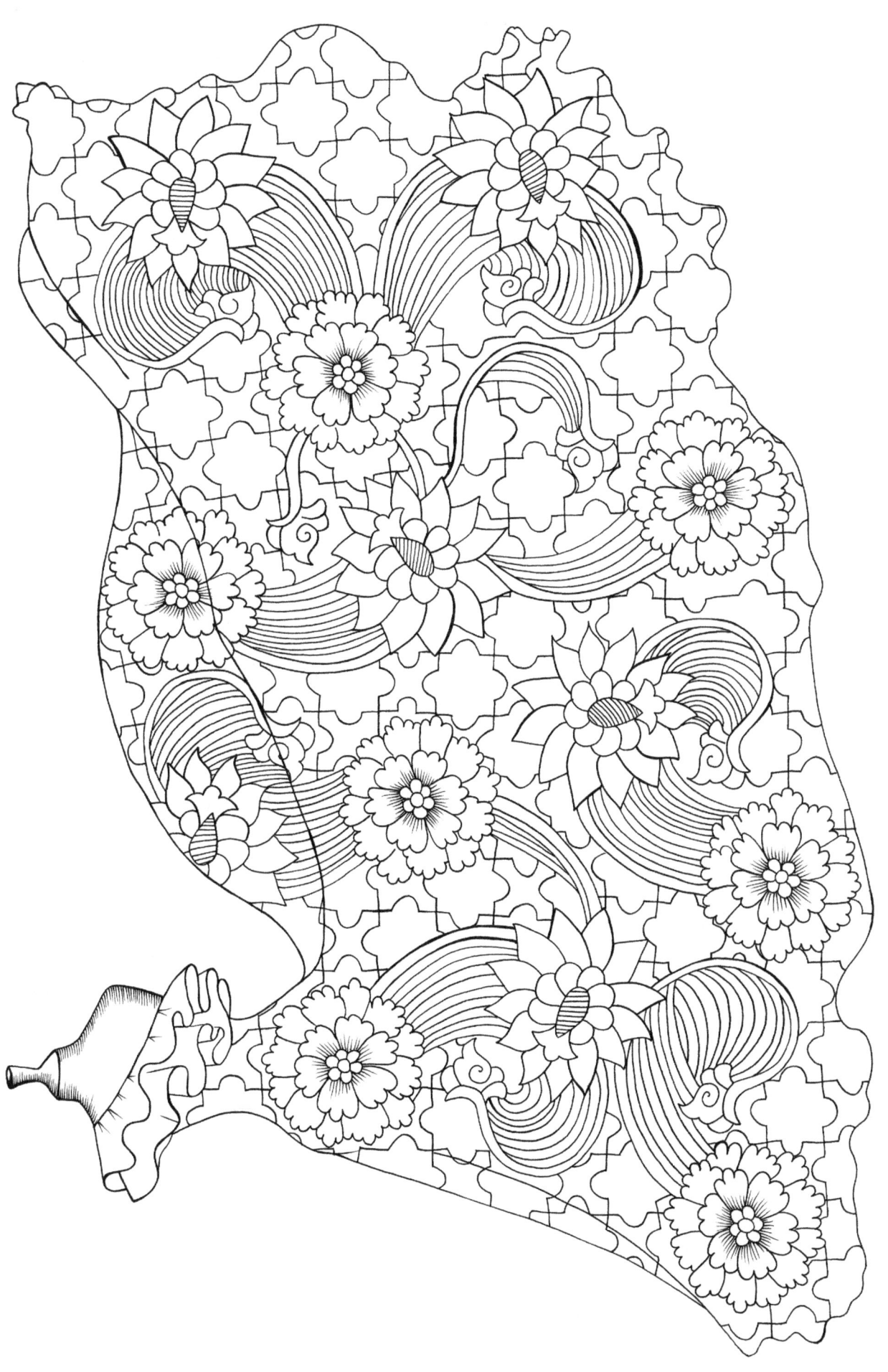

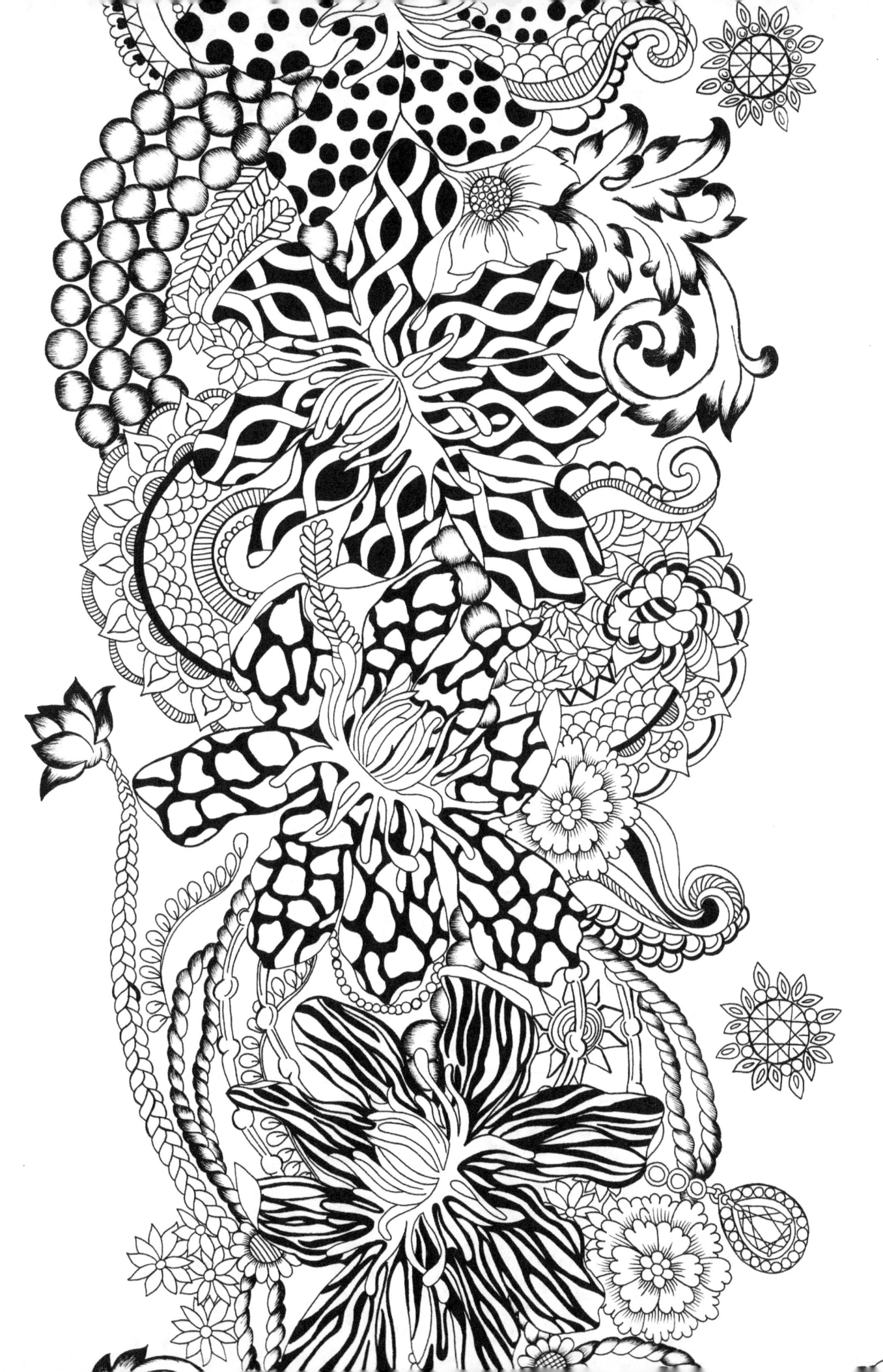

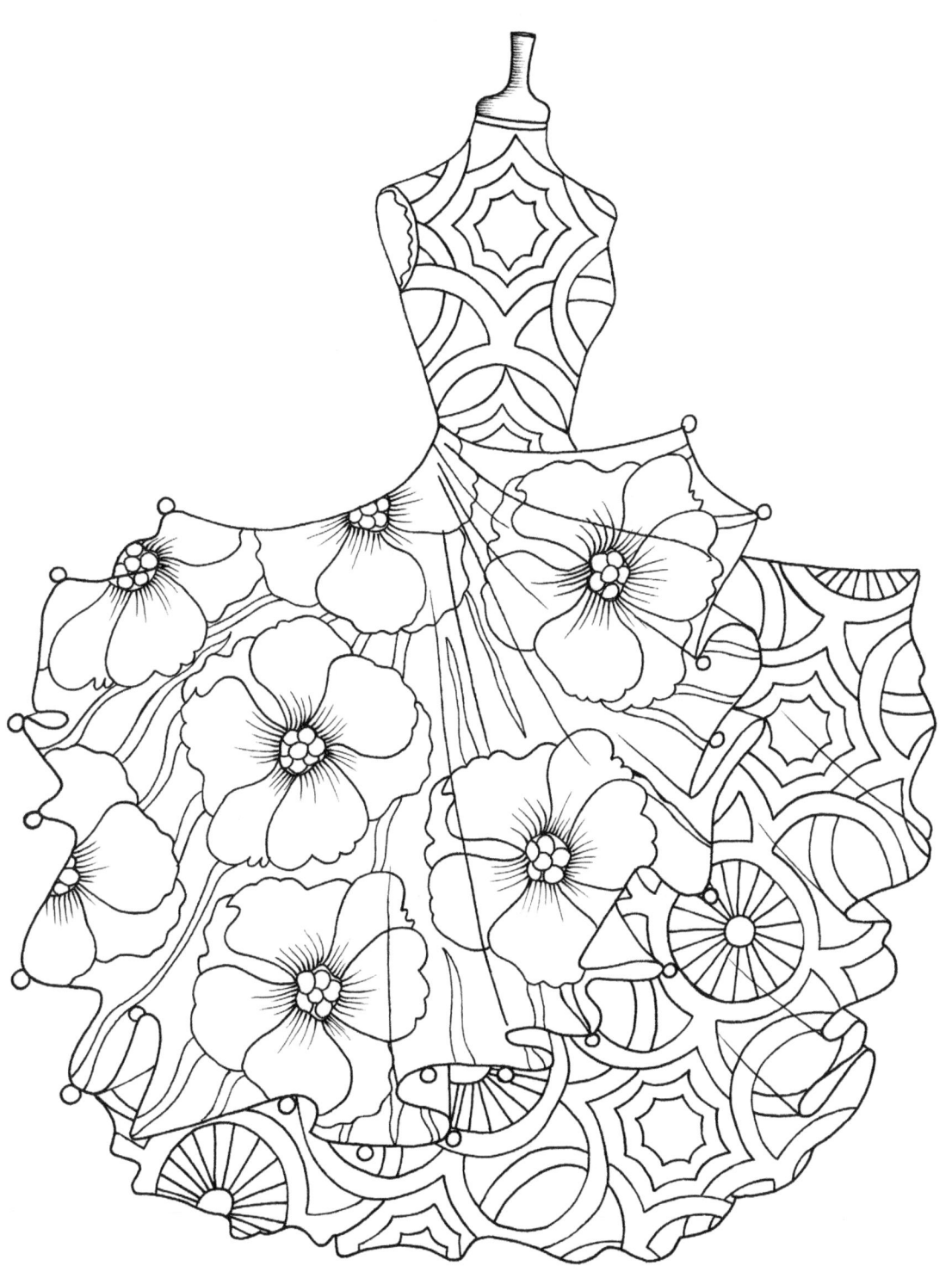

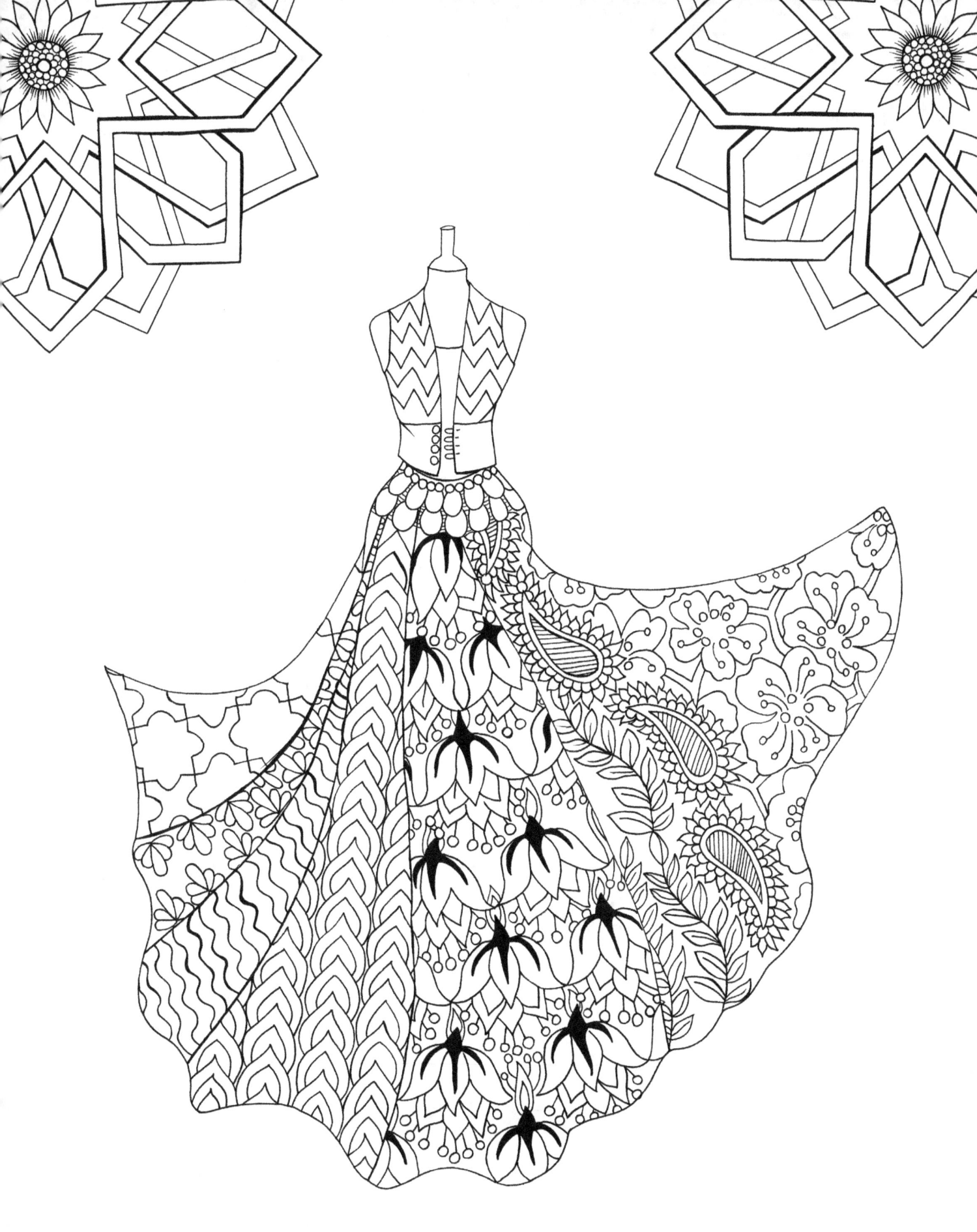

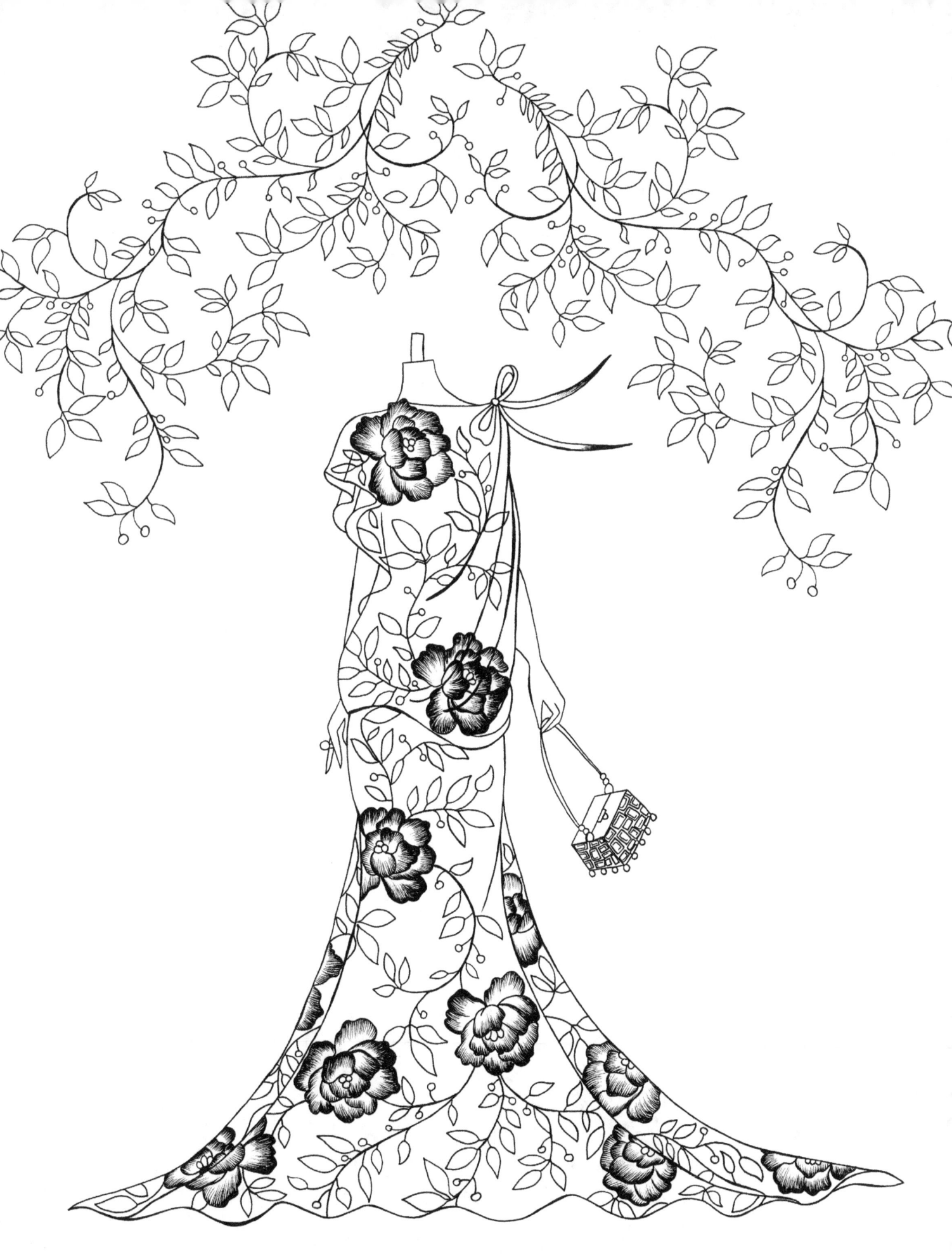

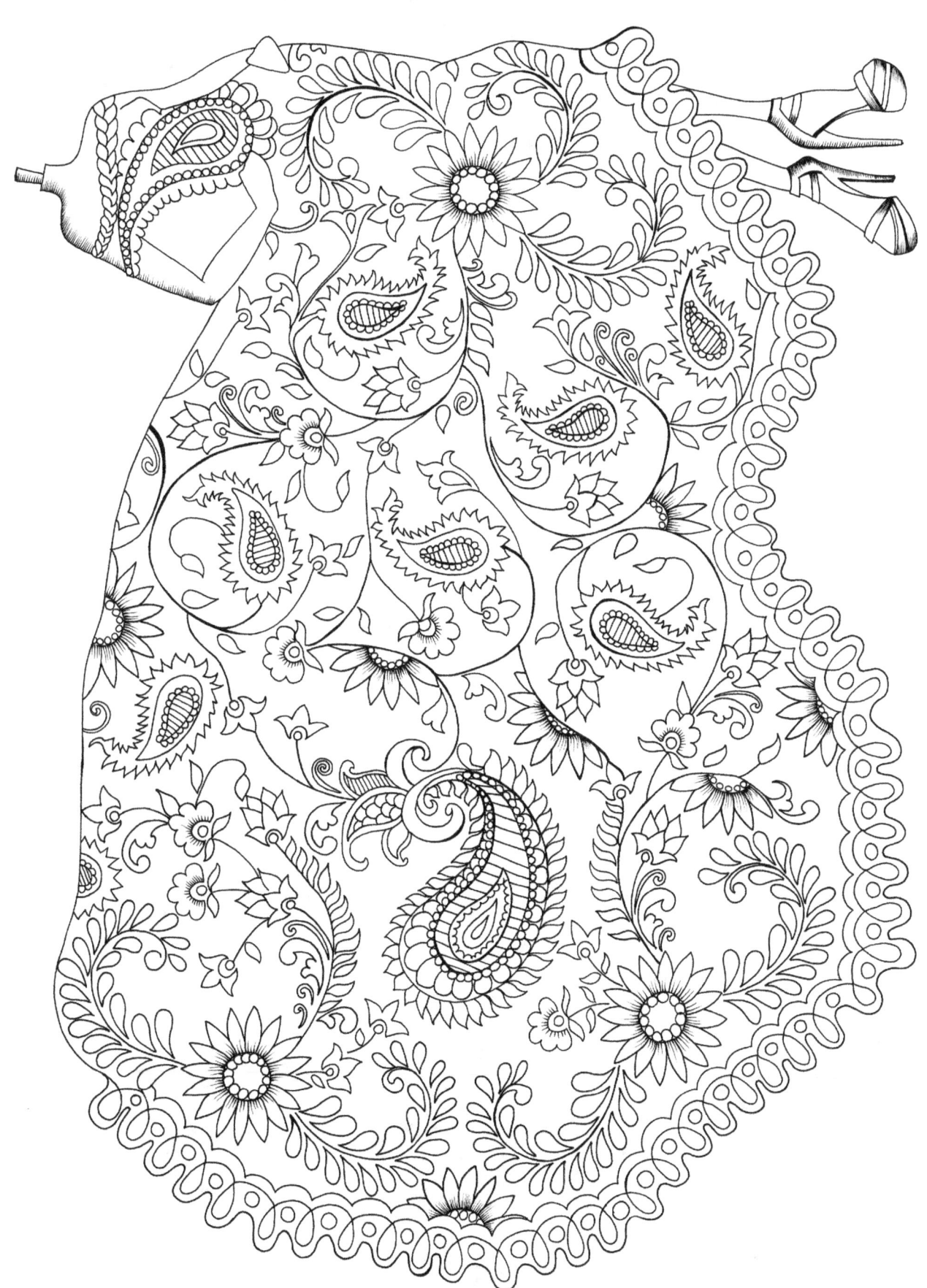

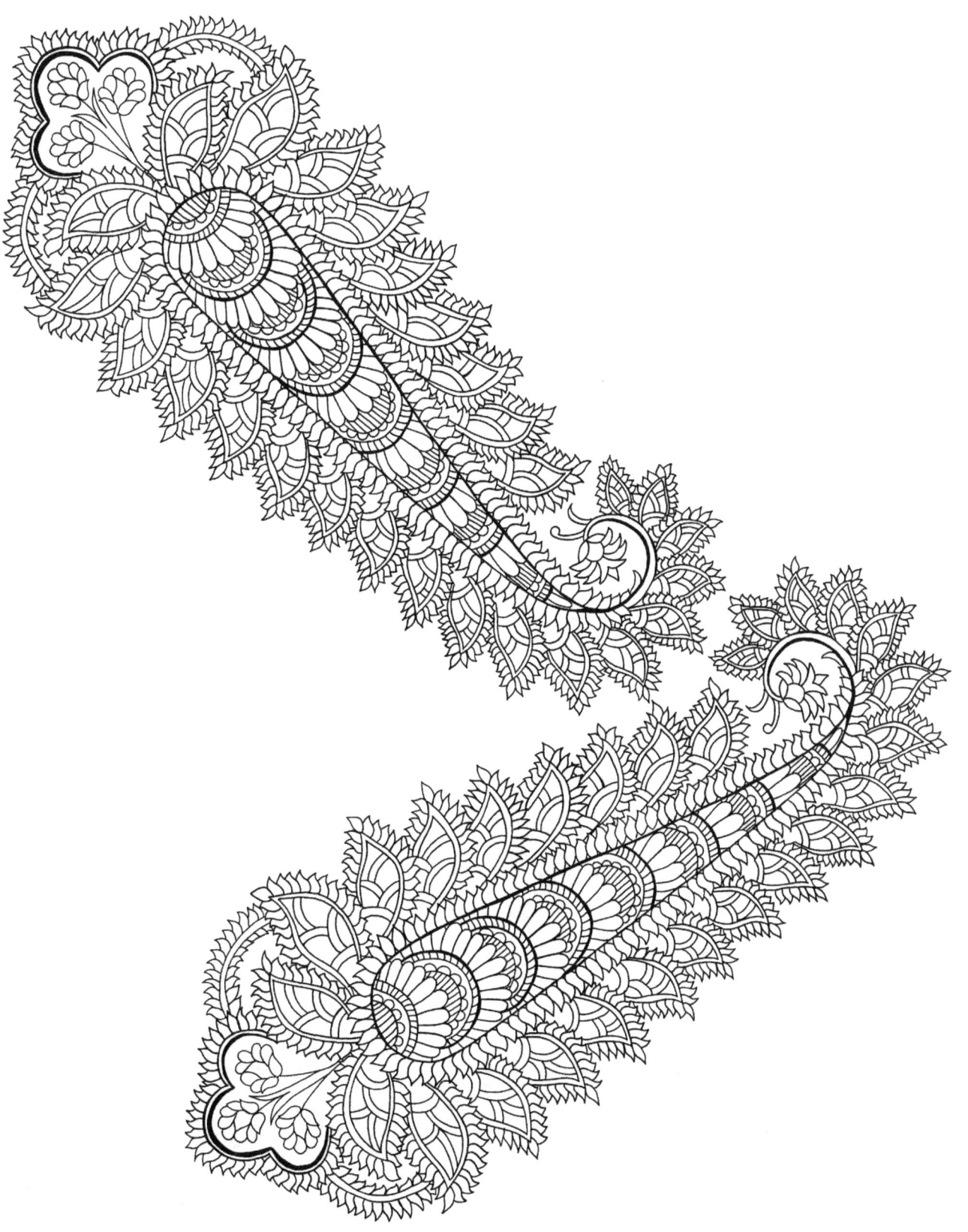

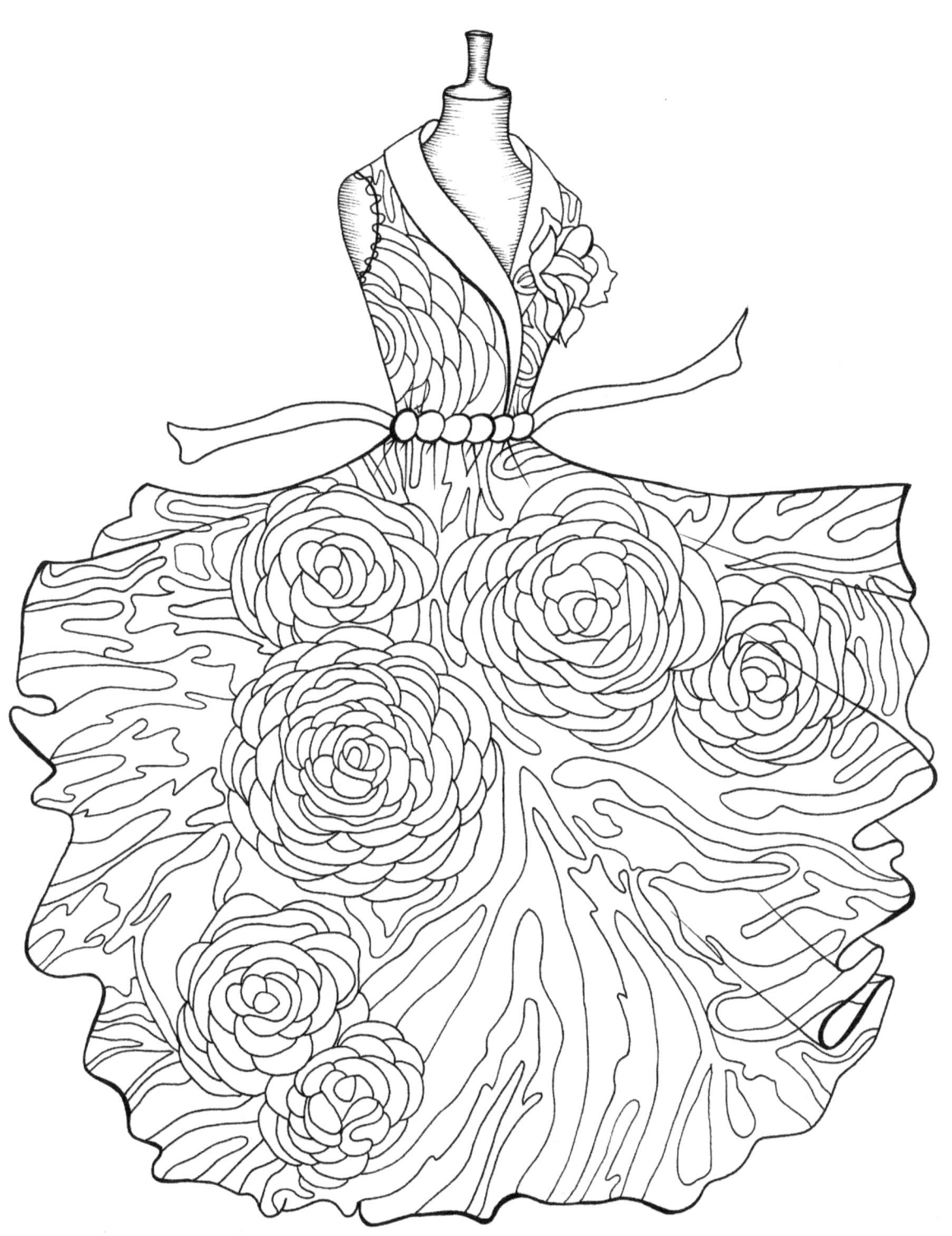

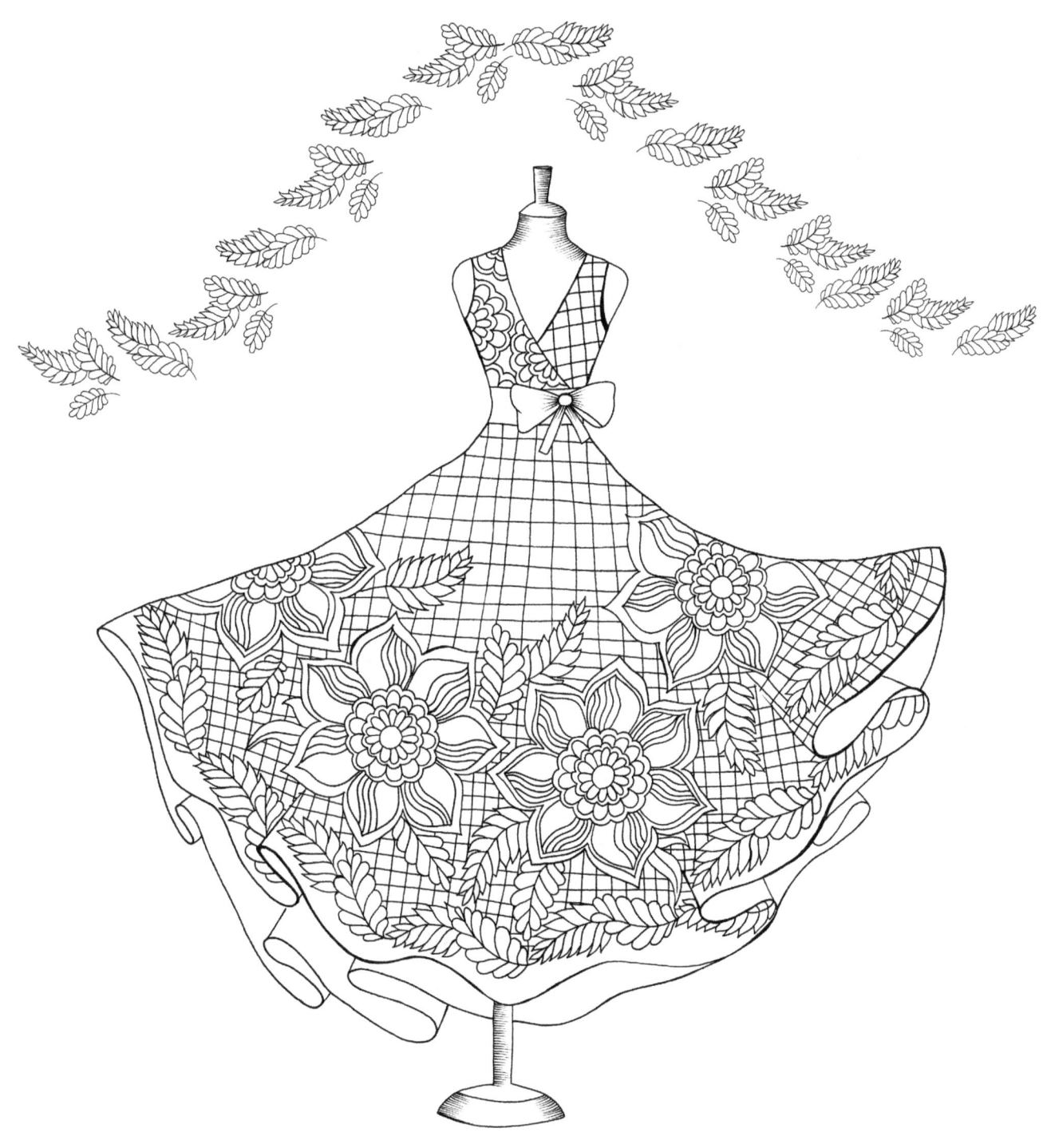

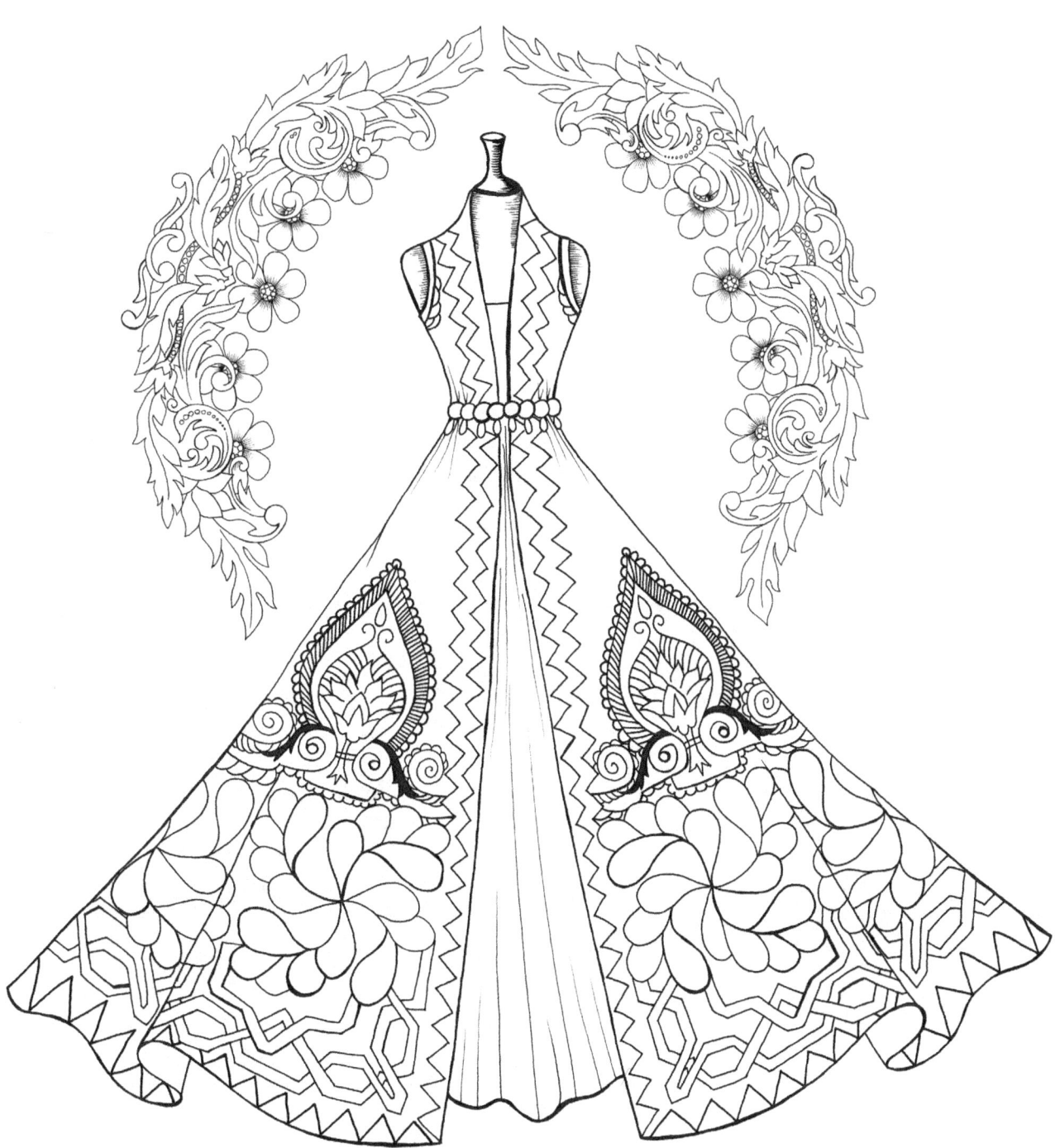

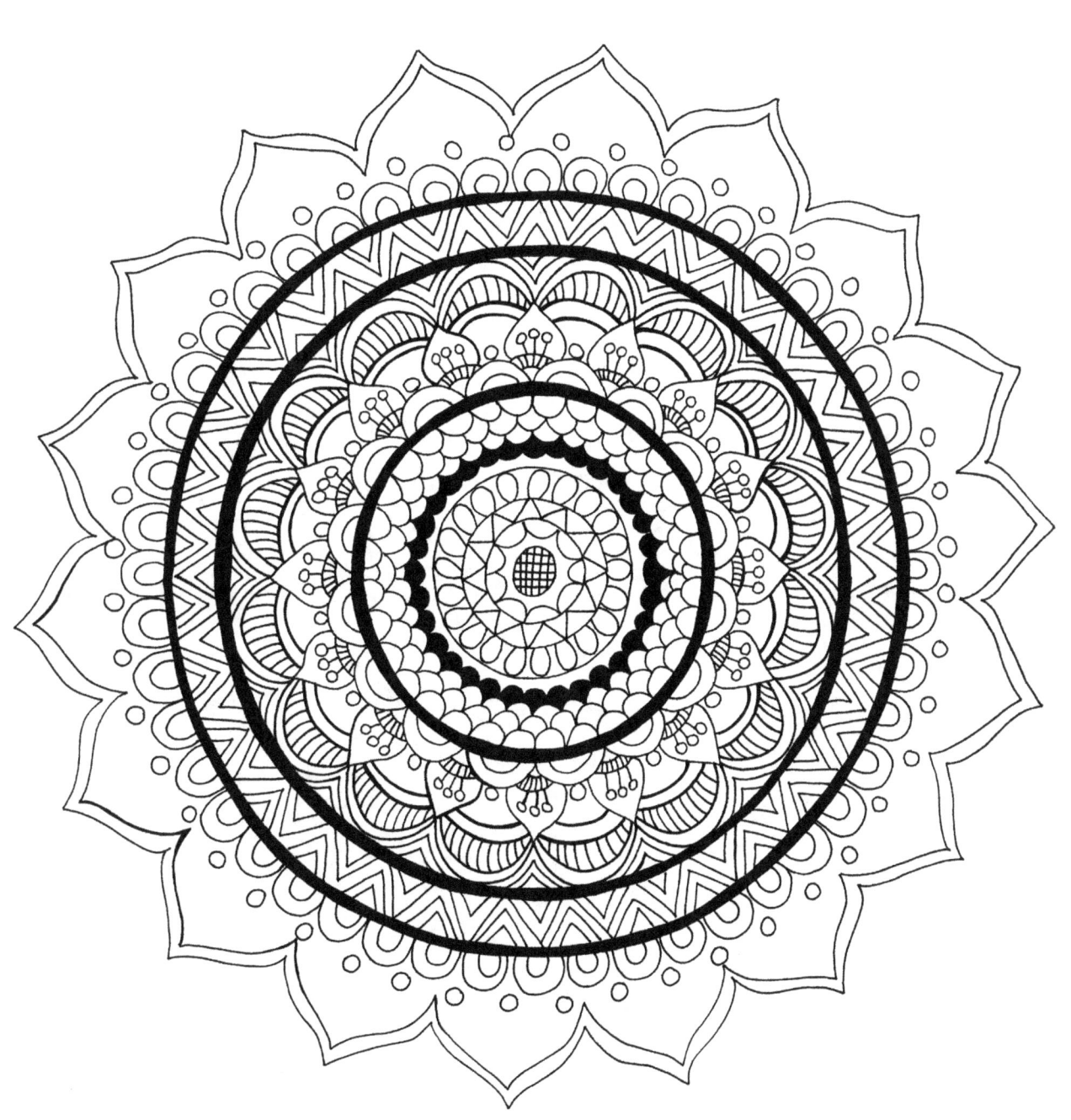

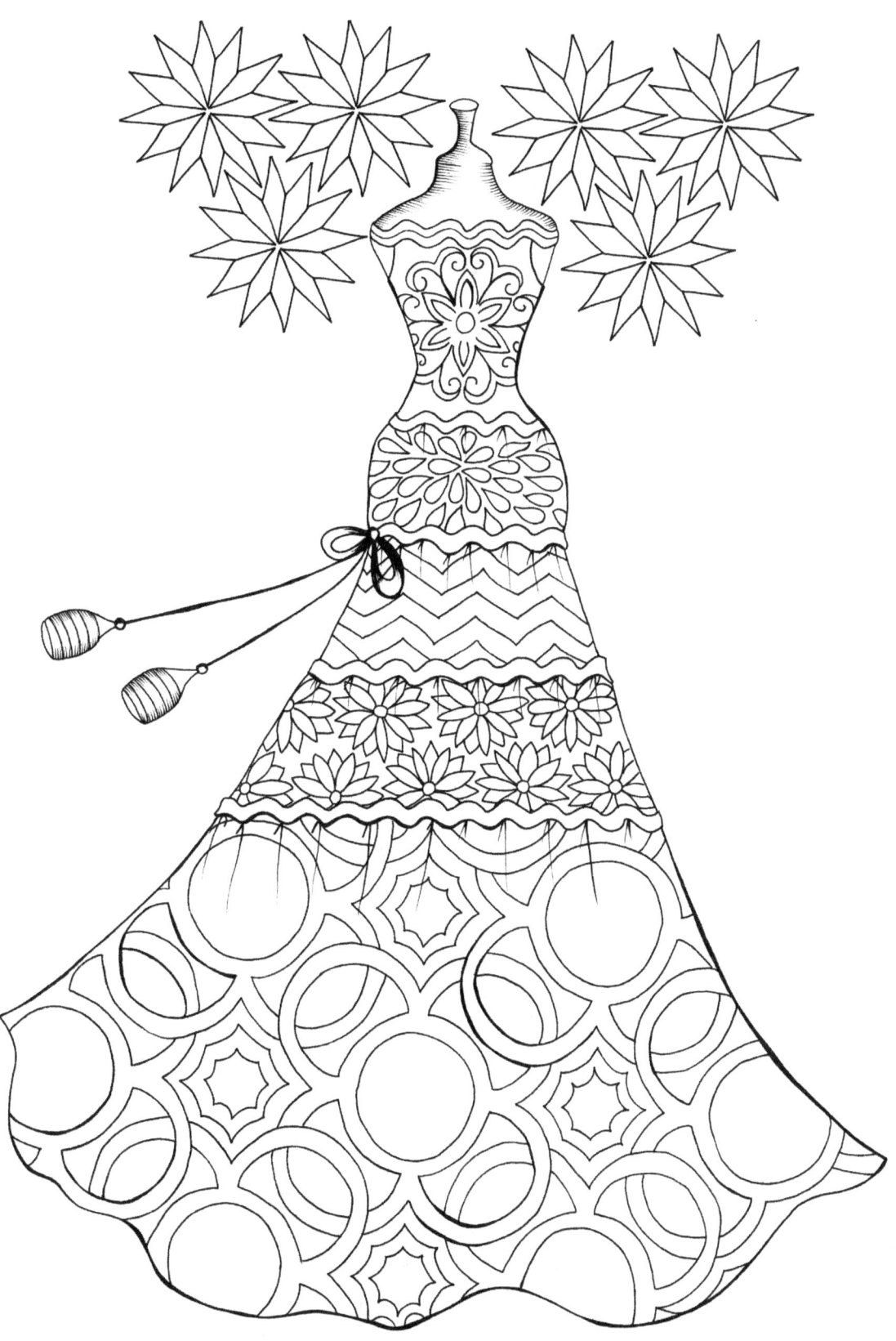

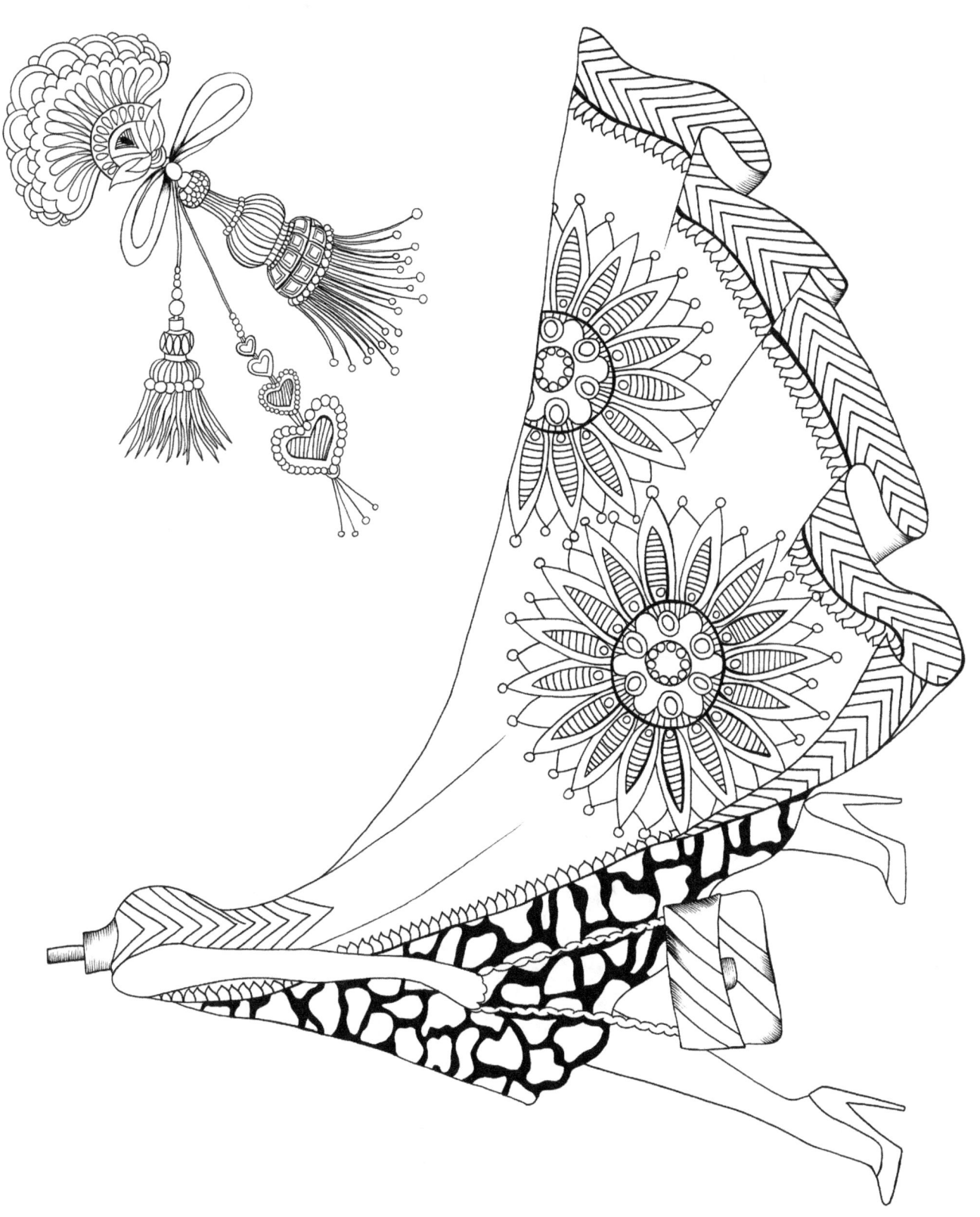

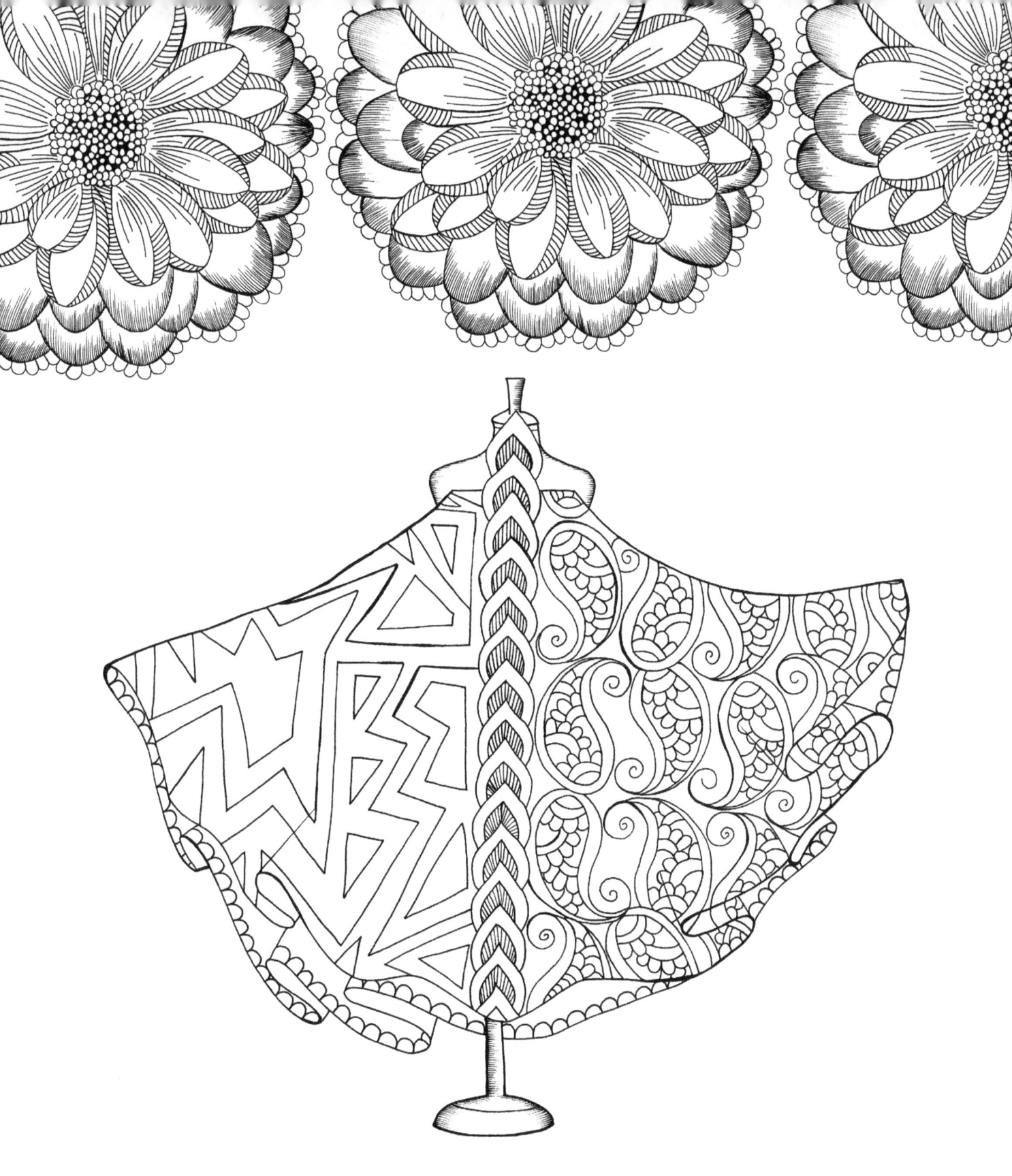

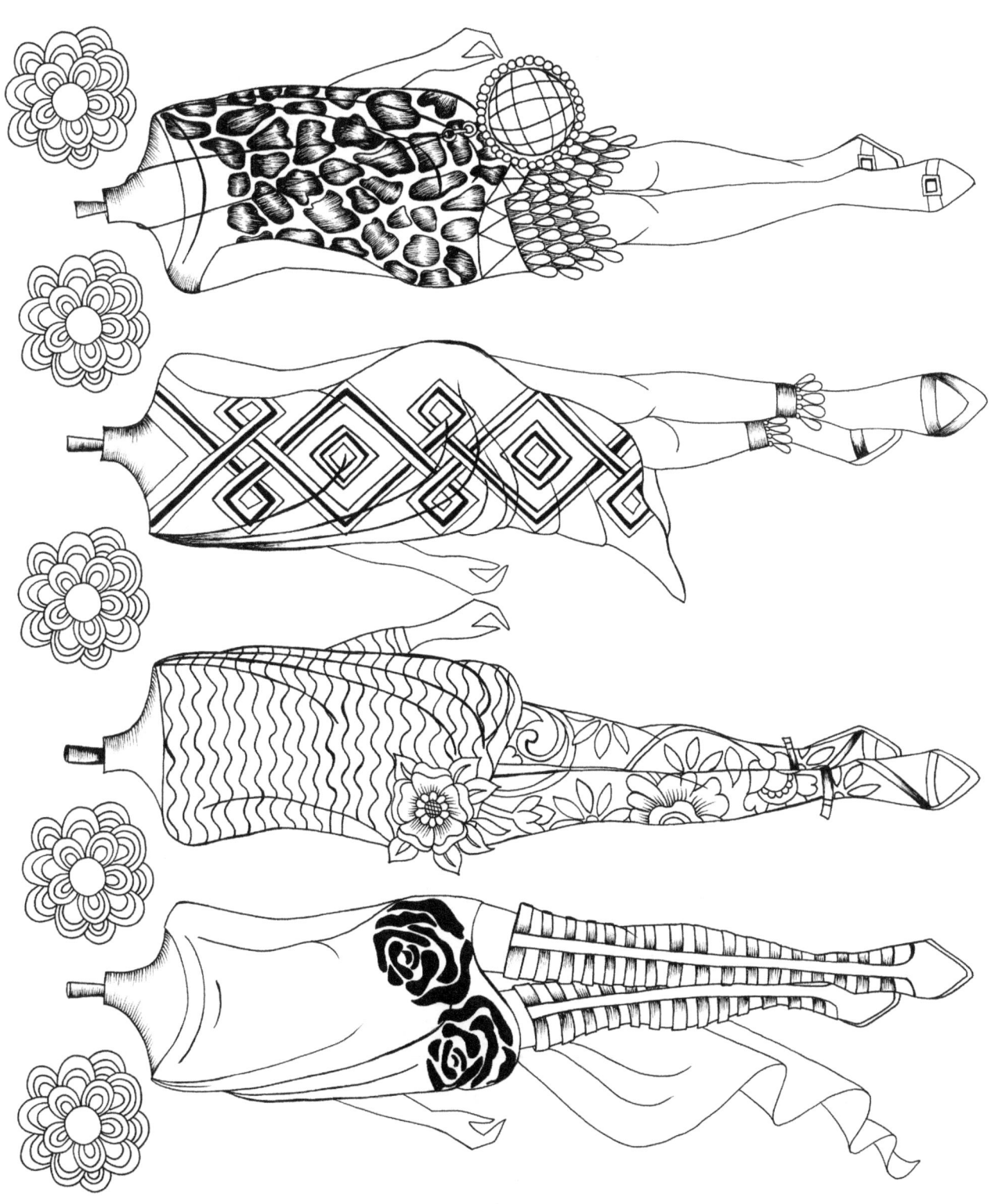

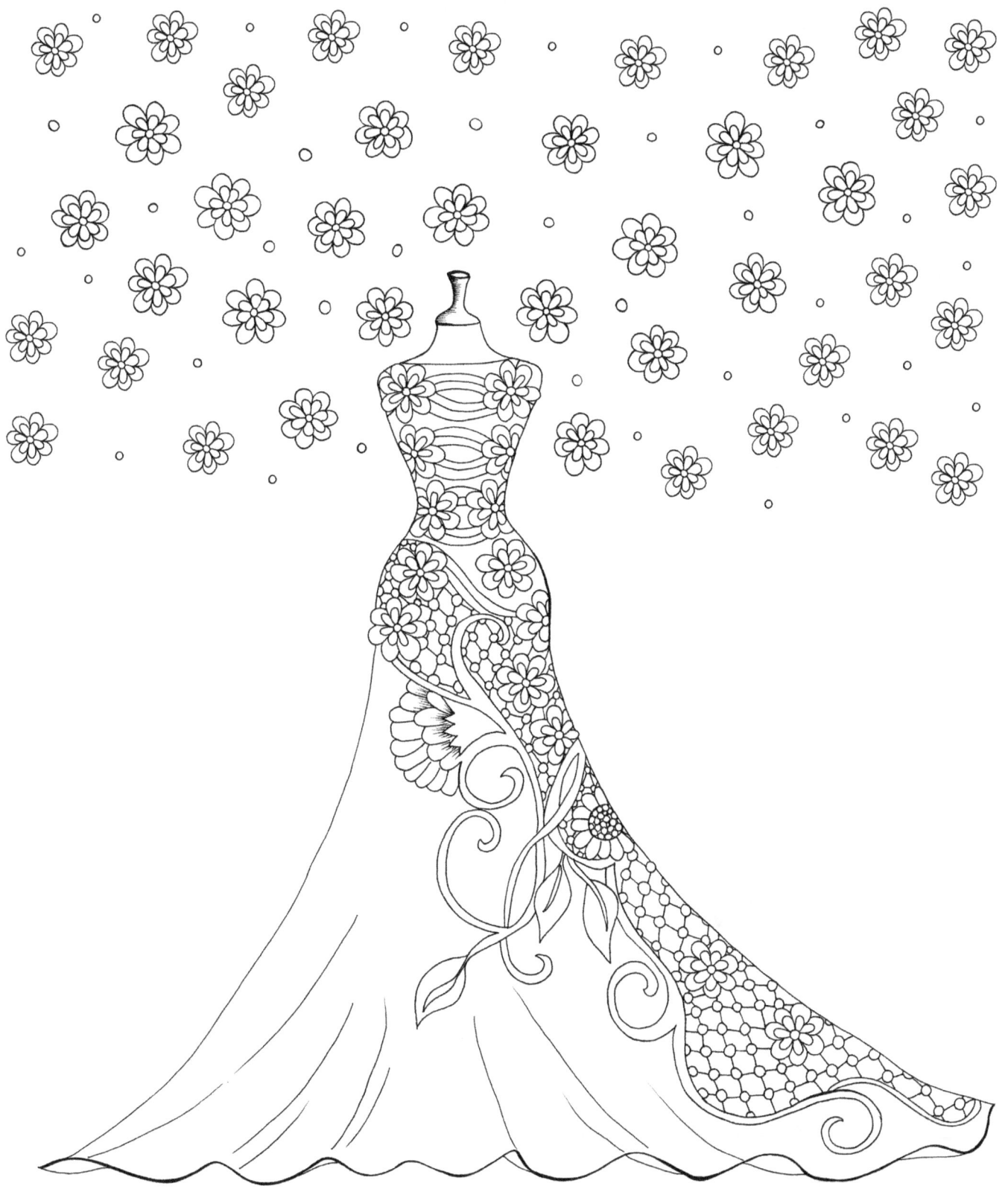

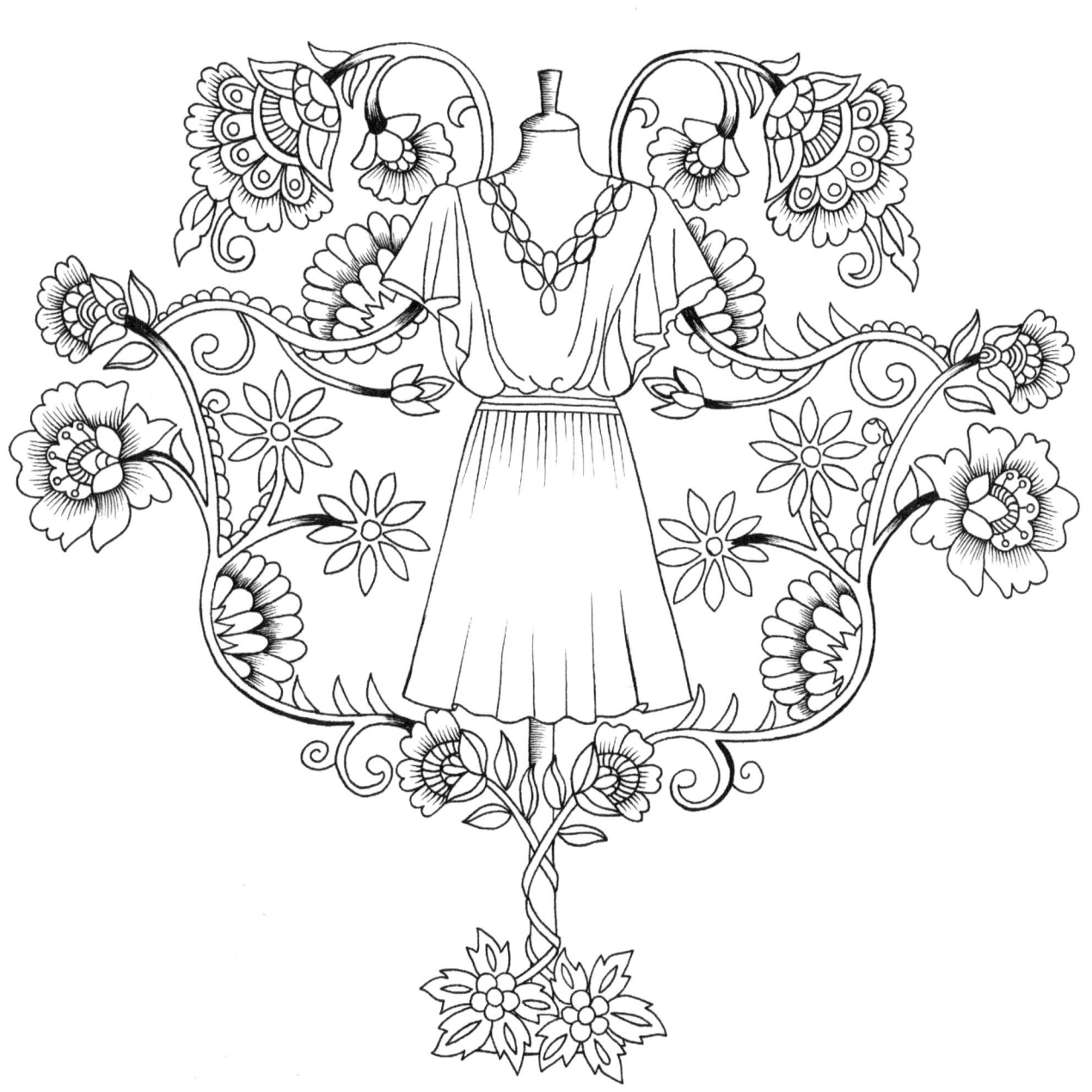

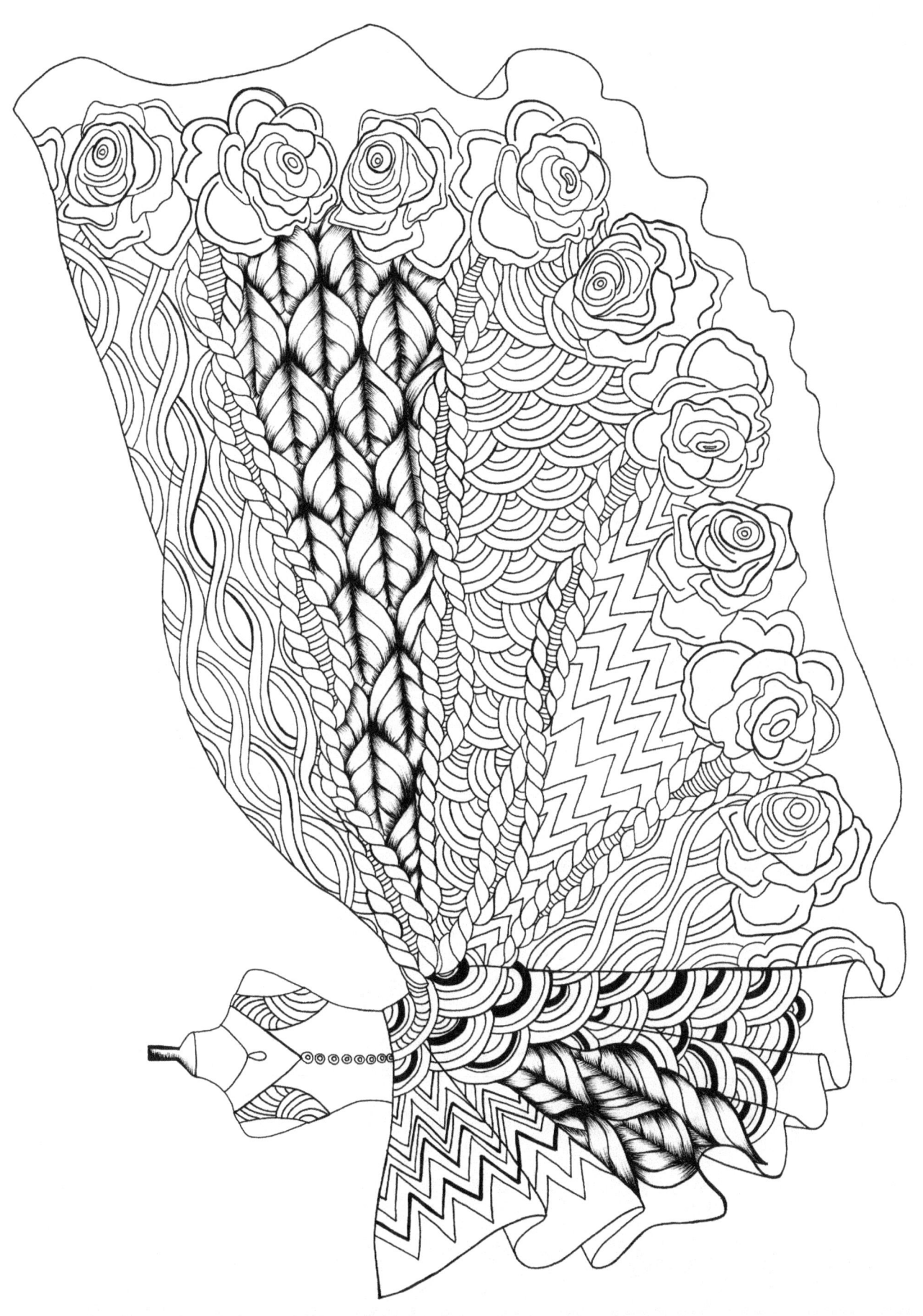

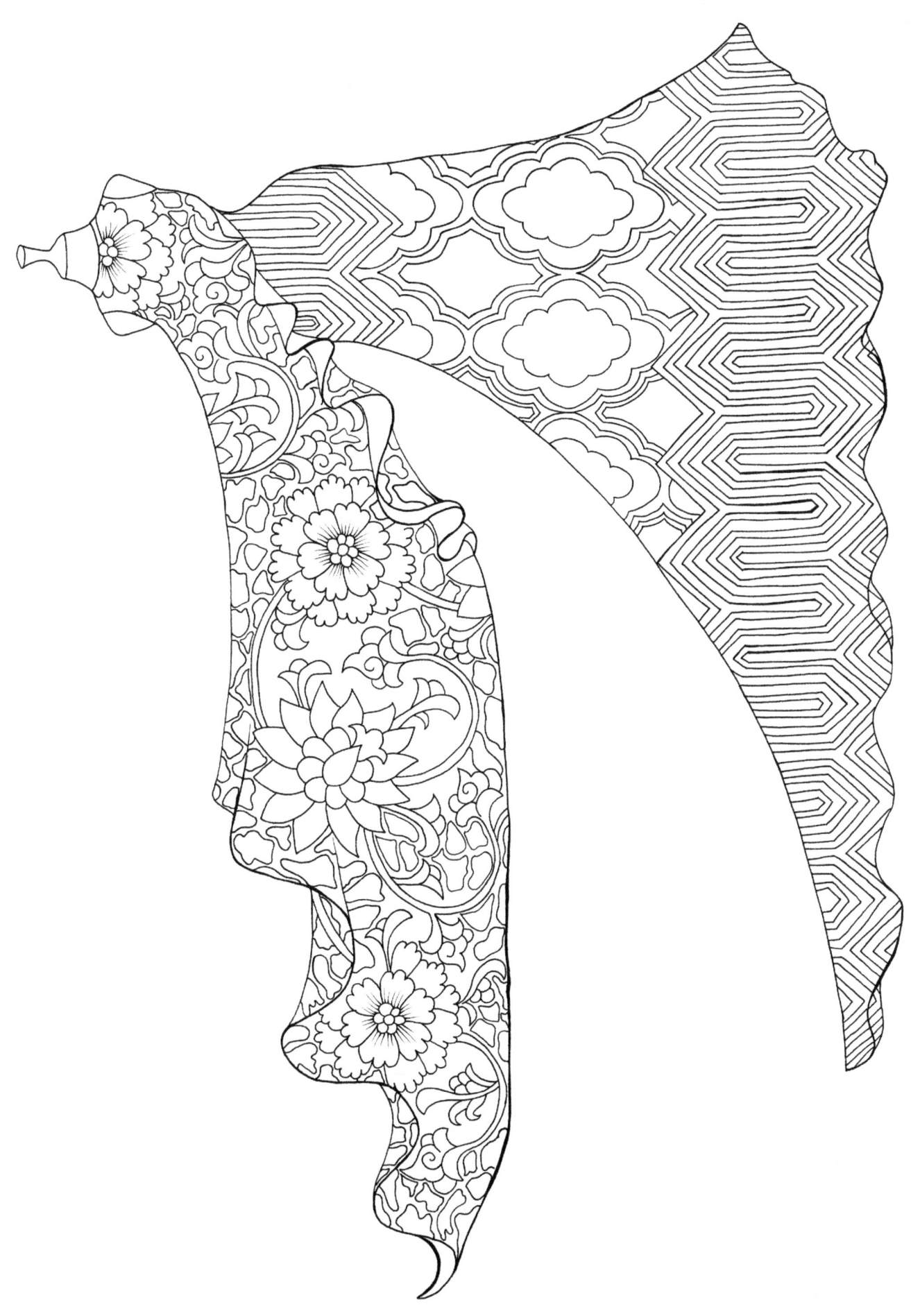

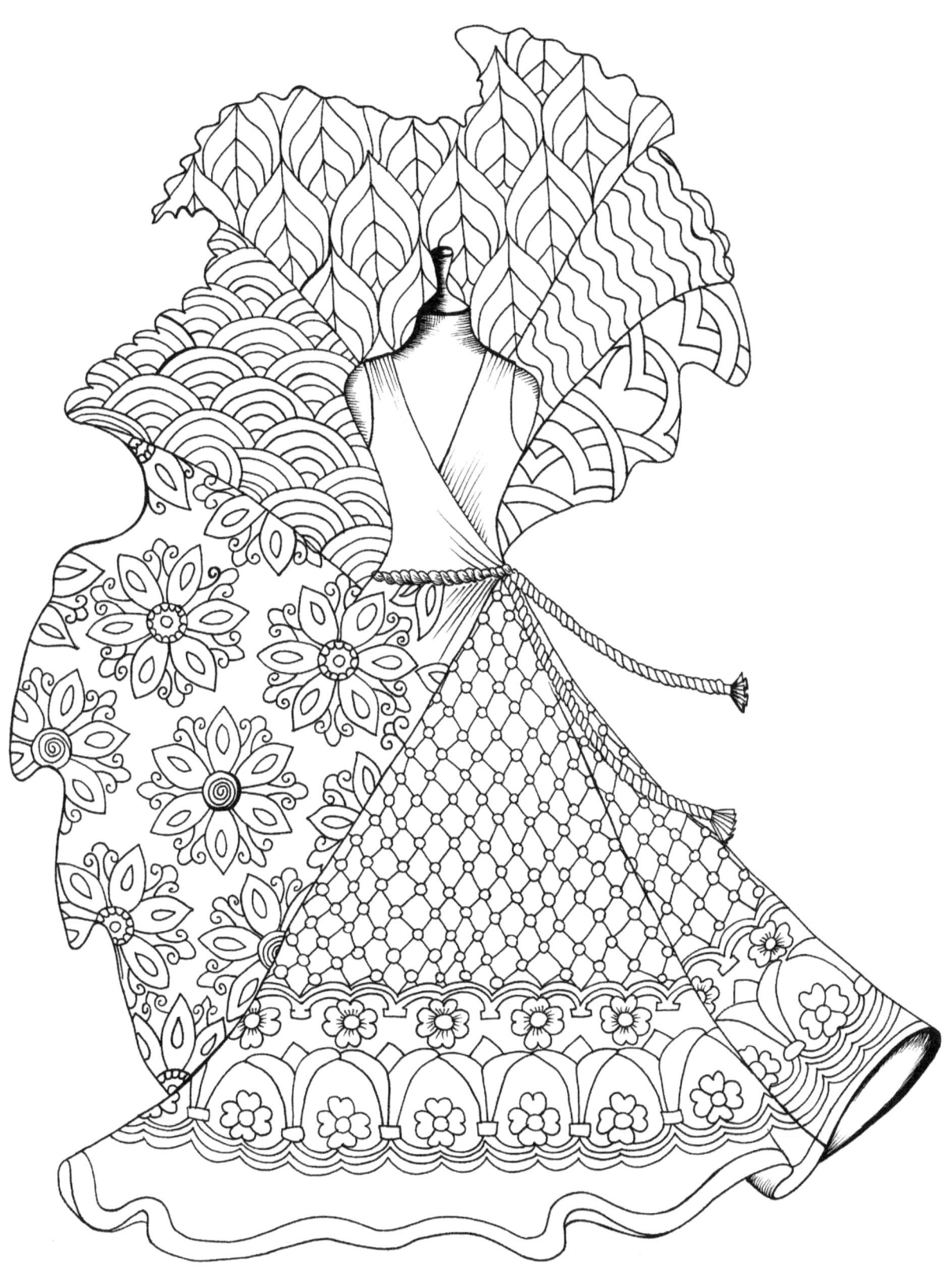

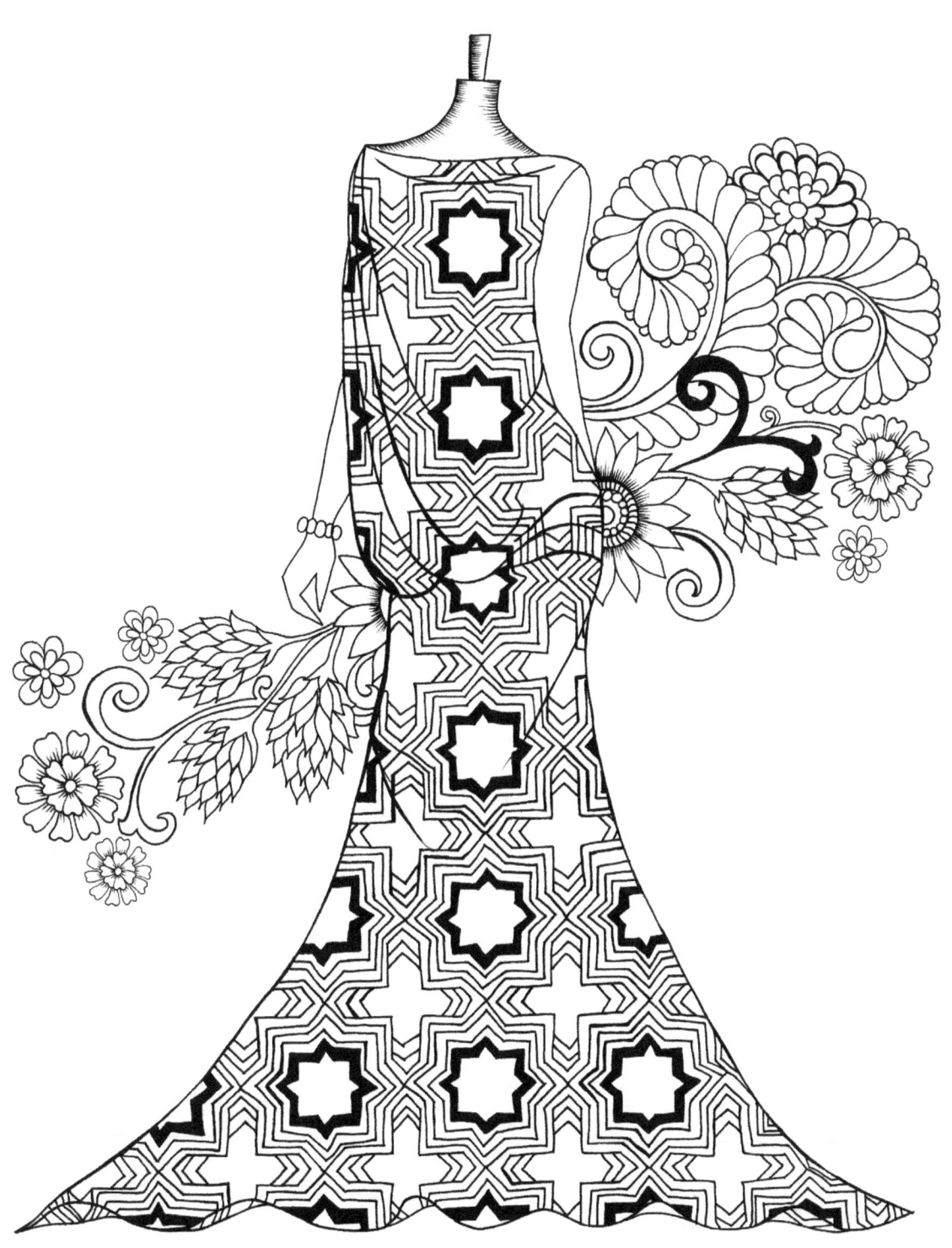

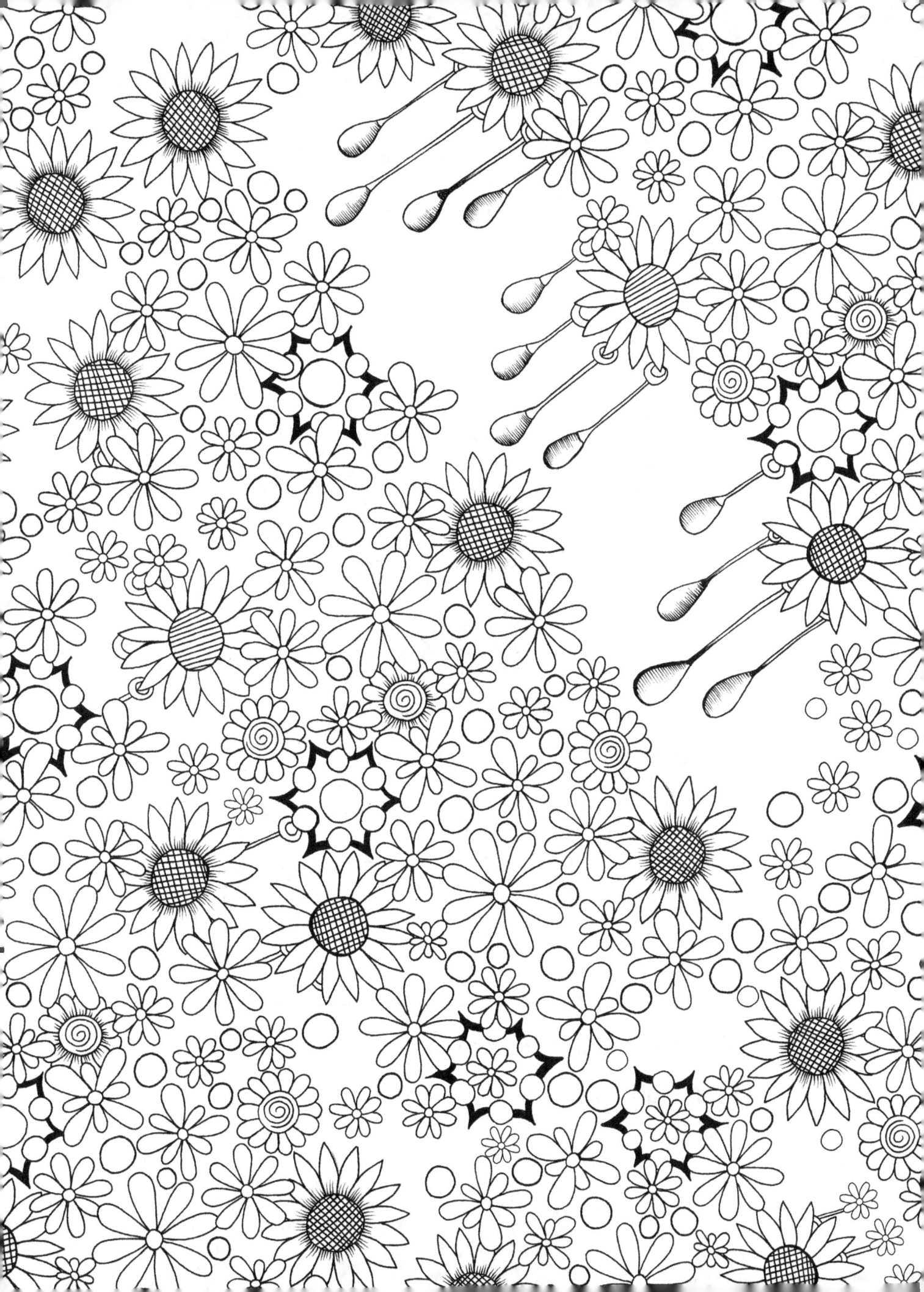

I hope you had fun coloring this book.
If you want to get in touch or have feedback
please visit my website to contact me.

Website address is www.mehwish.me

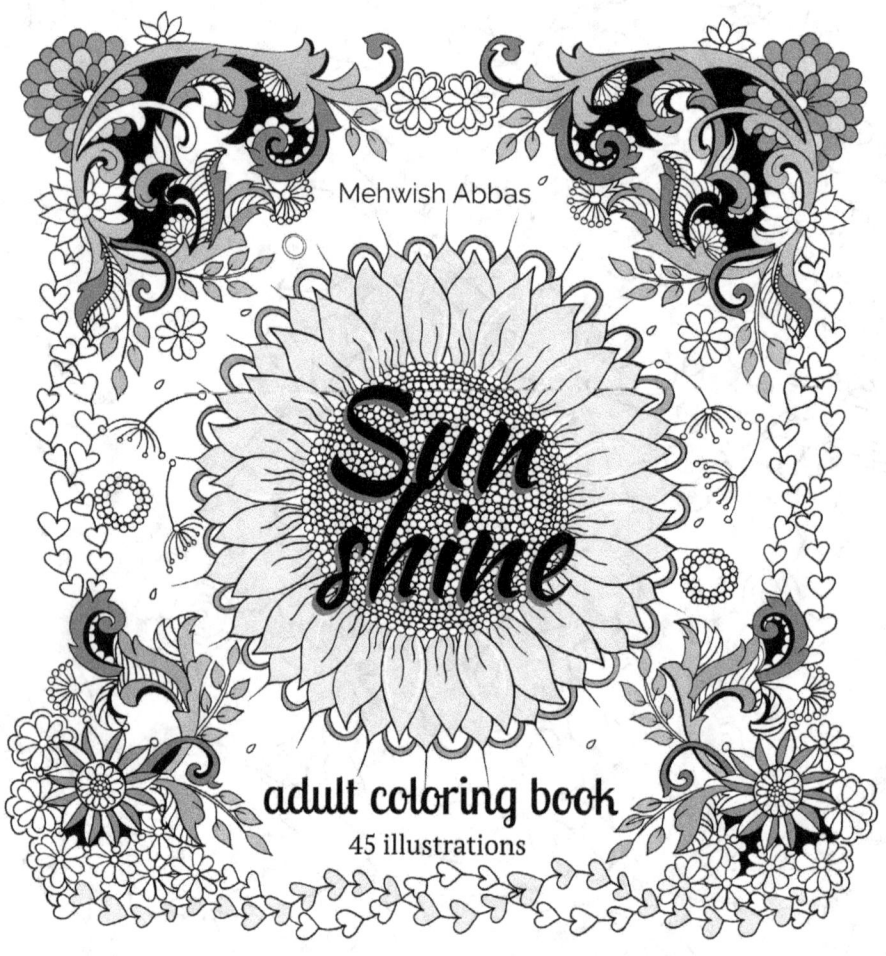

Sun Shine is my second adult coloring book.

You can buy it now from Amazon here

https://goo.gl/UAPjSG

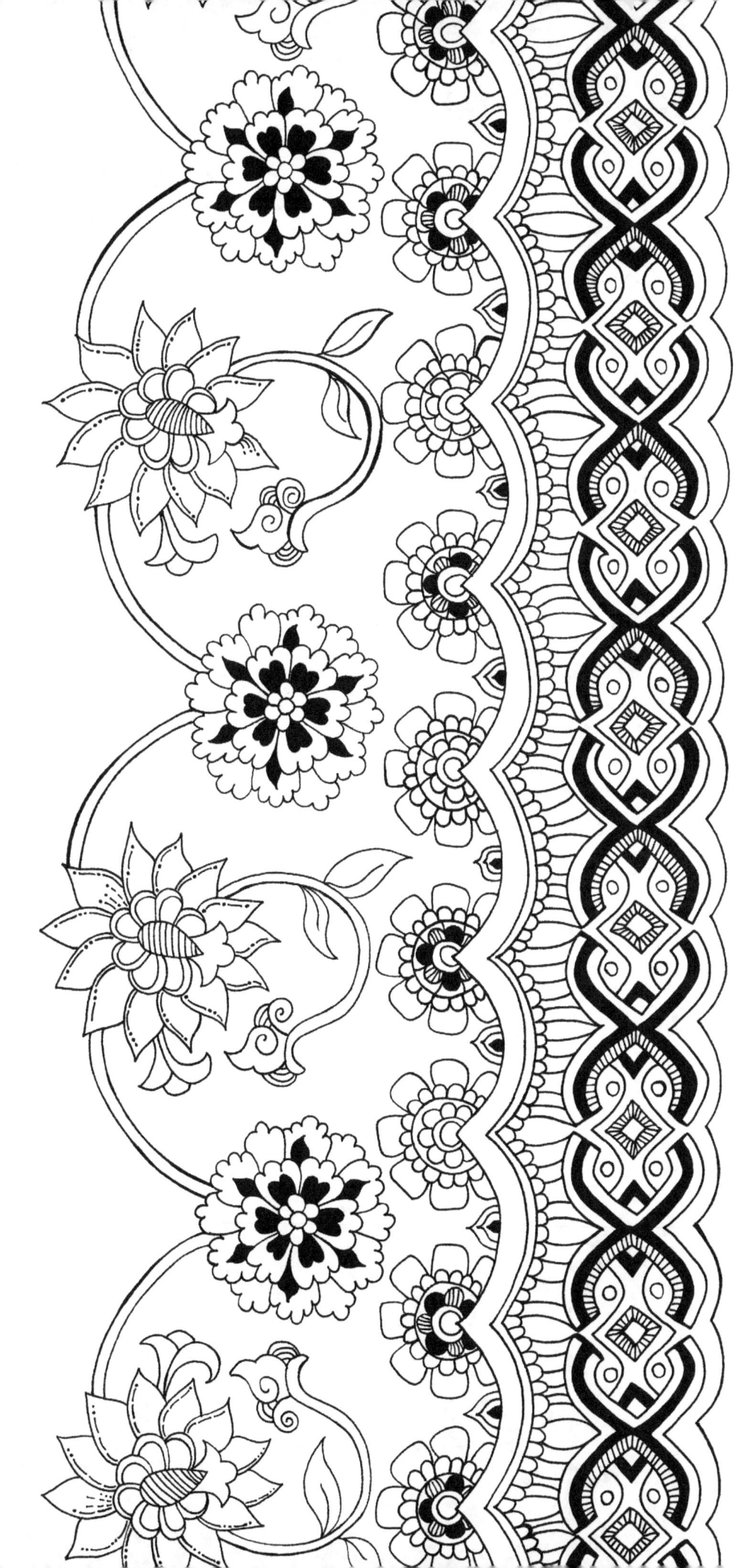

www.ingramcontent.com/pod-product-compliance
Lightning Source LLC
Chambersburg PA
CBHW081113180526
45170CB00008B/2831